When Mama Can't Fix It

Evelyn Goff

Copyright © 2010 Evelyn Goff

ISBN: 978-1-60383-368-4

Published by:
Holy Fire Publishing
717 Old Trolley Rd.
Atten: Suite 6, Publishing Unit # 116
Summerville, SC 29485

www.ChristianPublish.com

Cover Design: Jay Cookingham

Printed in the United States of America and the United Kingdom

Dedicated to the memory of my Mother
Martha (Tiny) Speer

A Loving Wife and Mother, who was truly an
inspiration to her family.

Table of Contents

Chapter One

Sweet Dreams

Little girls are made up of sugar, spice and sweet dreams. Growing up, you probably took a few trips down the lane that carried you away to fantasyland too. Daydreaming, you were a princess just waiting for the day that your prince charming would take you away. Played out on the stage of your mind, maybe you stared into the deepest, most beautiful eyes of this imaginary gentleman, who would become the love of your life. Taking a stroll on a nice summer day, with a gentle breeze blowing through the air, you felt his touch upon your shoulder. At other times, you imagined him holding you in his loving arms, or you squeezed his hand every so tightly. Sweet words were shared between the two of you, as you strutted about playing house. Oh yes, in the land of sweet dreams, life was really grand.

Adorned in the most gorgeous white gown, with all its frills and glitter, fantasy took you down the aisle of a lovely church. As all eyes were fastened upon you in all your glamour, your eyes were fixed upon the handsome prince, who was waiting for you. Tickling your ears was the sound of music playing "Here Comes the Bride" as you slowly took each step in stride. The ceremony ended with a kiss as your lips met his. Hand in hand you marched back down the same aisle, as the two lives had been joined together. In your world of sweet dreams, this day had been rehearsed many times over.

Hidden underneath this world of make believe are true desires aroused by human nature. Yearnings for true love and companionship captivates the heart of even a small child, which God instilled within the human race. After God had created Adam He addressed the issue of loneliness versus companionship. "And the Lord God said, it is not good that the man should be alone; I will make him an help meet for him." Genesis 2:18 He then created Eve, thereby providing Adam with a companion. From that day forward, an ignited flame of love has brought men and women together in holy matrimony.

God created and designed the institution of marriage, and then He blessed it and called it good. "Whoso findeth a wife findeth a good thing, and obtaineth favour of the Lord." Proverbs 18:22 Of course, the word wife is interchangeable with husband. A woman finding that life long mate in the man of her dreams is also wonderful. Marriage is a blessed favorable gift from the Lord, a special treasure, not to be taken for granted. The wedding vows are more than the fulfilling of a dream. They are a scared ordinance, to be taken very seriously, not haphazardly.

Sharing all of your dreams with this special someone who you will hold, love and cherish throughout your days on this earth adds a sweet aroma to life. Combining your hopes and dreams with his goals and ambitions and striving for a common ground will be exciting, and rewarding, but also very challenging. This can sometimes be where sweet and bitter come together. Each one gives a little and takes a little.

Don't allow compromise to be a bombshell that burst your bubble.

Along with dreams of Mr. Wonderful and a beautiful wedding ceremony with all the lovely festivities, visions of marriage led you to a nice little quaint home. Located in the land of fantasy, this home was built with nothing more than sweet dreams. Each imaginary trip that you took to this place left you simply awe-struck at the wonder of it all.

But, once the wedding day has moved from dreamland to reality and you and your wonderful groom arrives back from a romantic honeymoon trip, attention must be turned toward the making of your real home. To say that you are now settled into your new home with your new husband is a wrong perception. Girlfriend, you are in the home building stage not settled stage. "Every wise woman buildeth her house: but the foolish plucketh it down with her hands." Proverbs 14:1 Failing to build the home will create chaos instead of a peaceful settlement. Blocks, wood, and nails, may be the building materials to build a house, but not a home. A home environment is built through your relationship. Building a home is not found in sharing a house, but sharing in one another's lives. Sharing hopes of the future together, as well as helping to carry each other's heartaches.

All of your dreams came true, in the magnificent castle of your imagination. As your mind drifted off into wonderland, stepping inside this home sent a shiver up your spine. Scented with an aroma of pure joy, you breathed deeply, enjoying the lovely fragrance. Sheer happiness decked the walls of this wonderful place. Peace and contentment captivated your heart. But, if home is the place where dreams are made, then home cannot be left to chance. Just as a blueprint is drawn up before a house is built, God who is the finest architect of all wonderfully designed the plans for the home.

Love must be the foundation, which your home is built upon. Amazingly falling in love sent a tickling sensation up and down your spine, and butterflies fluttering in your stomach. His picture seemed to be permanently sketched in your mind, because you certainly couldn't think of anything other than him. But much more than warming your heart and touching your emotions, love is genuine caring and unselfishly attending to one another's needs, being patient with shortcomings and forgiving of mistakes. It has been said that love is blind; the blindness must be in overlooking one another's faults. Love is also being committed to a person. Stay committed to your dreams by staying committed to the man of your dreams.

Since building the home is achieved by building a loving relationship, maintaining the home hinges on maintaining the relationship. A good solid bond with one another can still crumble if left unattended. Each partner going their own separate way and losing themselves in their own little world may cause a crack to form in the foundation of the marriage. Of course, as the marriage goes, so does the dream. Patching the crack begins with each partner making time for one another again. Time invested in each other is an investment made into your marriage. Keep the home fires burning because; flames not sparked will eventually burn out.

In the fairytale story of your pretense world the word submission did not occur. But looking at God's plan, you will find it nestled right next to the word love. "Wives, submit yourselves unto your own husbands, as unto the Lord. For the husband is the head of the wife, even as Christ is the head of the church: and he is the saviour of the body. Therefore as the church is subject unto Christ, so let the wives be to their own husbands in every thing. Husbands, love your wives, even as Christ also loved the church, and gave himself for it." Ephesians 5:22-25

Domination by the husband to boost his ego was never God's plan for the submitting wife. The husband, who is selfishly demanding that his wishes be fulfilled without any regard for his wife's wishes and her best interest, is out of line with God's order. Making decisions for his family, the husband's devoted and cherished love for his bride, along with her wishes and needs should forever be at the forefront of his mind.

Submission does not mean that the wife has no input into the marriage. Submission acknowledges that you are a team, and every team needs a leader. Therefore, the husband should value the opinion of his wife. God created Eve to be a helper for Adam. As a helper to your mate, voice your ideas. Discussing matters of the family together, is not only allowed, but is necessary for unity in the home. But, in the world of submission, if husband and wife cannot come to an agreement and no

11

compromise is to be found, then the wife is to submit. Submission takes on a more positive ring instead of a negative tone if you understand that your husband is sincerely and lovingly attending to your needs and concerns.

As chief decision maker, the husband carries a heavier load than that of a submissive wife. Decisions made may be a big boost or a major let down to his wife. His children may rise to a level of great things or may suffer a decrementing blow, based on decisions of the household. Instead of sitting idle, the submissive wife should ever be in prayer for her husband, asking that the Holy Spirit lead him, and that he be filled with divine wisdom.

The rule of submission does come with an exception. Loving God with your whole heart and soul, submitting to His commands by walking in obedience to His word takes precedence over the husband's wishes. If submitting unto the husband means breaking one of God's laws, then your first allegiance must be to God. For instance, suppose a husband ask his wife to pack some heat, walk into a bank, and demand cash, by all means, toss submission out the door. Strong opposition and refusing his request would be the only wise choice to make. Submission would be breaking the laws of the land as well as the commandments of God.

Deception never entered the door of your make-believe home. Neither should it enter the door of your real home. Honesty within the marriage is a binding force, holding two hearts together. Sly tricks up your sleeve may end with a waterfall of tears falling from your eyes. Walking out the door behind trust and integrity will be happiness and peace of mind.

In a house, the chief cornerstone is designed to support two adjoining walls. Allowing Jesus Christ to be the chief cornerstone of the two lives that have been joined together adds a support to the home. During the storms of life, when everything seems to be reeling and rocking, Jesus will be the stabilizing force that holds the home together.

Along with all the dreams of dating, a lovely wedding, the perfect home, floating into the land of fantasy, was a picture of a precious little baby, calling you Mommy. From paper dolls to Barbie dolls and all other sorts of dolls, you played and dreamed, imagining the day that you would be cuddling your own little one. As you wrapped dolls in blankets, visions flashed before your eyes of the day that you would be wrapping a blanket around your precious bundle of joy, wondering would it be pink or blue. The imaginations continued as you dressed and undressed your little dolls umpteen times a day. Oh how sweet the visions of sitting in a rocking chair, baby held close to your bosom, while you fed and burped that little baby. This world of make believe is perfectly normal. Your world of sweet dreams was nothing more than natural born instincts being played out through your imagination.

After creating Adam and Eve the first thing that God did was to bless them and give them a command to be fruitful, multiply and replenish the earth. Intimacy within the marriage serves as a binding force uniting the couple as one, entwining their innermost being as an inseparable molecule, as each enjoys an expression of love and pleasure with each other. Conception of new life is also a God ordained purpose of such intimacy. God divinely placed within human nature the desire for intimacy as well as the desire to bare children. Most women experience a deep-rooted urge and sincere longing to become a Mother. However, a few women may find life quite rewarding without the addition of children in her life.

Just as marriage is a blessing from the Lord, so are your children. "Lo, children are a heritage of the Lord: and the fruit of the womb is his reward." Psalm 127:3 "Happy is the man that hath his quiver full of them." Psalm 127:5 O, what joy is bestowed upon a family at the birth of a newborn! As a baby grows, the excitement of the newness may wear off, but may the joy of your child never loose its luster. In the midst of problems, which by the way were not apart of the dream, may your heart still overflow with love and joy for your children.

In His design for the home, the master architect laid out the plan for child rearing. Joshua said it best with his proclamation "As for me and my house, we will serve the Lord." Joshua 24:15 As parents, you must set the stage that Jesus Christ is the center of the home, and that your household will live accordingly. Your children need to see a love for Jesus exemplified through you.

God assigned to you an obligation to teach and train your children in the word of God. "And these words, which I command thee this day, shall be in thine heart: And thou shalt teach them diligently unto thy children, and shalt talk of them when thou sittest in thine house, and when thou walkest by the way, and when thou liest down, and when thy risest up." Deuteronomy 6:6-7 The word of God should ever be before you, established in your heart so concretely that the word is cemented into the very depth of your soul. Your children should hear you speak the word, as well as see you live by the word. Teaching them to have a holy reverence for the Lord by the words you speak as well as your actions. If your children follow you, where will you lead them? Giving them one set of guidelines to live by and then watching you live by another most definitely sends the wrong message. Teaching your children and mentoring them in building their own intimate and steadfast relationship with Jesus Christ should be your primary focus. Any goal less than that mark should not be acceptable.

Pray and ask that the Holy Spirit be released unto the very depth of their soul. Protecting and guarding the word that has been planted is a divine work of the Holy Spirit. This seed will grow into full fruition as a result of the growth and cultivation of the Holy Spirit. How can a seed that has been withheld and never planted into the soil ever grow to maturity? Mama, your job is to plant the seed. Then watch the Holy Spirit nurture, protect, and grow the seed.

Mom, the perfect little angels of your sweet dreams probably did no wrong. Now, welcome to the real world! As that little innocent baby grows into a toddler, a little mischievousness will sometimes surface.

A little stubborn streak may arise, even turning into hard-core rebellion. Such issues left unattended will eventually lead to a life of perplexity for the child and grief for the parents. In the plans designed for the home, discipline was not just a suggestion; rather correction for the children was demanded. "Withhold not correction from the child." Proverbs 23:13

Discipline should never be used as an outlet to vent your anger, but to teach and correct the behavior of the child. "And, ye fathers, provoke not your children to wrath: but bring them up in the nurture and admonition of the Lord." Ephesians 6:4 Taking out your frustration in the name of discipline will most certainly provoke your children to anger. However, forsaking discipline will be a missed opportunity to properly guide the child. Helping the child to see the ill effects of their bad behavior along with encouragement to change their course should be the only intent of discipline. Scolding your child in a fit of rage does not encourage the child. Most likely, your raging fit will lower their self-esteem and load their shoulders down with a heavy burden.

While proper teaching and training is vital to the welfare of your children, some playtime is also essential. All work and no play is not only the making or a dull life, it also makes for a stressful life. While extravagant vacations may be out of reach for your family, much fun can be had for all through inexpensive outings. Games played indoors or outside activities can provide wholesome entertainment, as well as good quality bonding time for the whole family.

Every home needs some laughter, relieving the stress of everyday life. Now proper etiquette may frown upon talking and laughing at the table, preferring that everyone sit still and keep silent while eating their food. Certainly, there is a time and a place for such manners. But hey, my family has enjoyed many laughs together around the dinner table. We were not at some fine and fancy banquet or in a restaurant. Rather, we were family, at home, a place to kick the shoes off, sit back and enjoy one another's company. Munching on a meal together, enjoying a laugh or two, creating many happy memories adds a spice to life.

Following the divine master plan will not ensure that life will always be a piece of cake. In your sweet dreams, it never rained on your parade. But now that you are living in the land of reality, some days the freshness in the air seems to take your breath, as you embellish the beauty of the sunshine and smell the fragrance of the roses. On the other hand, some days brings a flood that no dam could hold back the rising waters, washing all of your sweet dreams away. Seemingly, the sun will never shine again. Remember, God holds the rainy days in His hand just as He does the sunshine.

Just because some dreams turned a little sour, don't stop dreaming. Set your sights on the visions that you have for your family and trust God to bring them to pass. Watching your young grow into baby steps, then into bigger strides, and finally marching down their own path of life, at times will be sweet dreams come true and at other times seemly you are living a horrifying nightmare. But, God is sweeter than your sweetest dream, bigger than your worst nightmare, and can fix what you can't.

Just imagine your life, a beautiful vase holding all your dreams and experiences. The story of your life can be told from inside the vase. One day the opening of the vase releases such a sweet fragrance into the air, as your sweet dreams lie before you. The beauty is simply breathtaking as the joys of life far exceed your expectation. Then the tide turns, and the vase is opened with a horrific odor. Puff, all your hopes have evaporated as a vapor of black smoke carried them off into thin air. Disappointments have snuffed out your dreams. Yesterday's laughter wiped away by today's tears of sorrow. Yesterday pride swelled your heart big enough to burst, while today's heartache will surely burst your heart. Harmony within the family may have been replaced with harsh disagreements. All the sweet dreams that would carry you away to live in a palace happily ever after have become a living nightmare.

Longing to gather up all of your sweet dreams and safely store them away again, your heart cries out as it searches for a way to fix the vase. Standing at a crossroads you gaze into the future, uncertain of the road ahead. At the same time you look back down memory lane. Some memories leave you relishing the beautiful moments, while others leave you wondering what went wrong. What shattered the lovely vase into pieces? Most importantly, can it be fixed? Mama, some of the pieces you will be able to fix and some you will not. But, every broken piece of your life, God can fix!

God was the creator of your lovely vase from the very beginning. "But now, O Lord, thou art our father; we are the clay, and thou our potter; and we all are the work of thy hand" Isaiah 64:8 He will turn your brokenness into an adorable vase again. Pouring into your vase by the hand of God will be new dreams that you never imagined. Instead of dry places, He will bring you to new rivers with crystal clear water. He will dry your tears, taking your sorrow and filling you with gladness.

Reshaped and remolded, your vase has been upon the wheel of the potter once again. Sanding the rough edges and going through the hot fire of the kiln was torturous. But once more, your vase has been polished into a beautiful shining piece of artwork, and life is sweet again. As you walk down the path of life, you will again smell the sweet scented perfumes as it flows over your vase that once was cracked and chipped, but has been fixed and refurbished by your creator.

Chapter Two

Beyond the Dream

While the man of your dreams may have swept you off of your feet, some of your dreams may end up being swept under the rug or thrown out with the dishwater. Heartaches and pain will cause some of those precious fantasies to float away in a fountain of tears. You may dream big and plan well, but life will still deal you an unexpected crushing blow from time to time. But, hand in hand with your mate at your side and allowing God complete control at the helm, He will steer you over the rough seas during the high tides as well as the low tides of life.

Some problems may be small and have an easy fix, while others will take the pressure point to a rolling boil. Some will be unavoidable, while others will be self-inflicted. Hasn't everyone gotten them self into a jam a few times due to their own mistakes? Blaming one another for a bad judgment call will only hinder the process of working through the situation and finding a fix to the misfortune.

Off to work you go. Hum, was that in the dream? The palace that you dreamed about did not exactly include coming home after long and tiring hours of work to a husband that also had a hard and grinding day. One of you is cranky and the other is grumpy. Now there is dinner to cook, a kitchen to clean, and laundry to do. What ever happened to the good life? You know that life that was in your dreams!

Well surely after all that work, there should always be enough money to pay all of the bills and buy all of the luxuries that you have dreamed of having. Far too many couples have chased that trail which leads to a deep hole of debt. High mortgage or rent, a house full of new furniture with all the accessories, all on credit of course, and car payments may not leave enough dollars for food and other necessities, not to mention emergencies. Struggling to stretch the budget, which seems to fall short month after month, will certainly stretch your nerves, test your patience and will most likely affect your marital relationship. Keep your financial obligations within the guidelines of paying bills, buying necessities, and saving for a rainy day. Oh, and one other thing, do not forget that paying tithes to your church should come first, as the Bible has instructed you to do.

Although, you may be wise as an owl concerning your finances, spending cautiously and diligently saving, you may not be safe and secure from ever suffering a financial hardship. Some major catastrophe could wipe out all of your savings with the blink of an eye. Not only can unexpected expenses take a toll on the family budget, but your sanity as well. Though your funds may be limited, God's resources are unlimited. Remember, He fed more than five thousand people with two little fishes and five loaves of bread.

As time marches by, one day you discover that a baby is on the way. Wow, what a thrill! Now the house is bustling with excitement. Much planning and preparation is underway. A nursery to be decorated, but first you must decide on a decorative theme, just the right colors to pick, and all the right accessories. Will it be a little girl or a big bouncing boy? Ringing in your ears may be just the right name for your little one, or searching through a baby name book, the majestic name may be dancing off of the page, or quite possibly you are inspired to give it the name of a special family member. Whichever method used, you will not stop until you are convinced that you have chosen just the right name for your baby.

As you eagerly await the arrival of your first child, time seems to drag by. Finally, the much-anticipated day arrives. Grabbing the suitcase that has been packed for weeks, then out the door you and hubby go. Riding to the hospital, all sorts of thoughts swarm through your head. Approaching the hospital, your emotions shift into high gear, running from love, joy and excitement to fear and great apprehension. In the visions of your mind, this scene may have played out many times. But, the intensity of the moment was never this big.

Upon hearing a cry, a tear may trickle from the corner of your eye. Covering the grimace from the suffering of childbirth, will be the glow upon you face as you look into the little face of your precious newborn. Holding this tiny infant in your arms carries you into a deeper dimension of love than your dreams ever could have carried you. Regardless if this new little bundle portrays more of the handsome features of Dad or is a reflection of Mom's radiant beauty, you are cradling the most beautiful sight that God ever created.

Mom, unlike the dolls of yesteryear from the world of make believe, this is a real live being, with a beating heart. Greater responsibilities now lie before you than you ever imagined. Problems like you have never encountered will also come along the way. While some will only be minor incidents that will suddenly disappear by the magical touch of Mama's hand, others will be a major crisis that Mama can't fix. Honey, you are not dreaming anymore, you are now living beyond the dream into reality.

Leaving the hospital, settling in at home with Mom, Dad, and baby is quite another realm of excitement. Neighbors, family, and friends rush over to admire the newest addition to your family. Never before have you felt so proud, as you do now, showing off this new little bundle of love.

All seems to be going well, and then suddenly one night the baby doesn't sleep, maybe doesn't look quite right. Reaching for the thermometer Mom rushes to check the temperature. You guessed it FEVER. Of course, this has to be at nighttime when the Doctor's office is closed. All your efforts to break the fever seem to be to no avail. Instead of going down, it only climbs higher. Rocking until the wee hours of morning, all the while frantically looking at the clock, anxiously waiting for time to call the Doctor and praying with every tick of the clock, Mom is on edge. Nights like this may sometimes end with a trip to the emergency room. Mama can't fix it, but surely the Doctor can.

As you adore the most gorgeous baby that you ever laid eyes upon, life's hopes and dreams expand well beyond the walls of your own desires and ambitions. The center of your world is not focused upon you anymore. Carrying you off into the future are high hopes and sweet dreams for the life that you now hold. Only a tiny, little infant, but big plans are already underway. Nothing but the best will do for this little one. Your wondering mind carries this child to the highest level of greatness.

After awhile, a baby crawling across the floor never brought such joy to your heart. Next comes walking and you gleam with pride as each step is taken. And then a few words are muttered. Soon a little vocabulary begins to develop. Listening to every little word, you suddenly realize that not only is this the most beautiful child ever, but the smartest one too! Surely he or she will do magnificent things is life.

On the other hand, you may be one of the many Mothers, which the birth of your darling baby was accompanied with tragic news. Something is horribly wrong with your child, no cure to be found, and no Doctor can fix it. As fear grips your heart, a huge lump forms in the throat, tears fill the eyes, and the pit of your stomach suddenly is attacked by a sickening sensation. Questions are coming at you faster than answers. Will my baby ever have a normal life? Are there any medication or treatments that can help? Or even worse, will my baby live? Mom, though you may feel that all of your dreams have now been shattered, in reality, they may have just been altered. Instead of living the dream that you once envisioned, life may have taken a different direction for you and your family. But, God knows every crook and turn in your path. He is ready, willing, and able to restore you to a new hope.

Although your child may have some serious illness, maybe a physical limitation, or possibly some mental challenge, this child is still a marvelous and wonderful creation of life. Your child was designed and hand crafted by the perfect creator. "For I am fearfully and wonderfully made." Psalm 139:14 As you carried this baby in your womb, the creator of all beings carefully and awesomely formed this little one into a unique individual. "Before I formed thee in the belly, I knew thee; and before thou camest forth out of the womb I sanctified thee." Jeremiah 1:5 Before the seed of this child was ever planted within you, the Lord knew and had a purpose for your little one. Neither disabilities nor incurable diseases are mistakes, rather opportunities for God to perform a miracle. God may choose to miraculously heal, or simply strengthen and sustain you and your family each and every day by His marvelous grace. Nonetheless, a miracle has been performed.

Tragically sometimes Mama's thrilling dreams of bringing her baby home is turned into the shrilling agony of death. Fighting back tears, one Mom shared with me the horror of losing her child at birth. Nine years have passed and she still choked up talking about it. Plans were set, the baby's room prepared, a diaper bag packed and Mom ready for the hospital. Hemorrhaging, Mom was suddenly rushed to the hospital the day before the scheduled delivery. In an effort to save the baby, an emergency cesarean was performed. Unfortunately, the baby did not survive. Instead of bringing home a baby to cuddle and caress, or to rock and sing lullabies to, this Mom had to come home and plan for funeral services.

Complete emptiness is how this Mom described her emotions. Stating that she never knew what it was to feel empty inside until that tragic day. She felt completely lost, utterly hopeless, and that her life had no meaning. Waiting was a crib that her baby would never sleep in. Empty bottles were only a reminder that she would never feed her baby. Staring her in the face were diapers never to be used. Precious was the clothing that the baby wore from the hospital to the funeral home. At night she slept clutching a teddy bear, which she dressed in those little clothes. Certainly, this was no scrape that Mama could put a bandage on and fix. For the first time in Mama's life, she knew that she could not fix what was broken.

In the midst of her sorrow, this Mama is also grateful. She gives thanks that her baby never knew pain. Her little one never shed a tear. The blessed assurance that her child is at rest with the heavenly Father brings consolation to her heart. In Mama's wildest imagination, this scene never crossed the screen. Even though she has two other children, an empty spot will always remain in her heart for the one that was lost. But, God has soothed the pain and restored her soul. Once again life has a meaning and purpose.

Mom, suppose that the birth of your babies brought the wonderful news that all is well. Breathing a sigh of relief, you bowed your head and thanked God. Along with being thankful for a healthy little baby, you even spoke a prayer of thanks for ten little fingers and ten little toes. Wonderful as life seems, you never could even imagine a crooked turn. A few earth shattering blows will still rock your world sometimes.

You may fret over a few flu bugs from time to time. A spike of temperature may even raise your eyebrow occasionally. But when the symptoms only worsen and the temperature continues to rise, Mama gets seriously concerned. But, if that bug that you think your child has turns out to be a critical diagnosis, maybe even life threatening, your world is suddenly rocked. Maybe your vibrant, beautiful and intelligent child is mangled for life from some horrible accident. Oh how badly you wish that you could come to the rescue and fix them back up again. But Mama can't. Mama, if you never face a critical illness or view the mangled up body of one of your children, you can still be certain that a few rocky roads will run through you beautiful garden of life.

While children grow physically, their mental capacity is also expanding. Exploring their own thoughts, their little minds will conceive ideas that clash with yours. Sometimes the broader their mind becomes the more their notions go against yours. While a strong determination has its advantages, it can also produce a rebellious personality. Of course the children of your dreams were all sweet and innocent. Dealing with a rebellious child simply was not in your plans. Now it seems that the harder that you try steering them on a good solid path, the more they seem determined to jump off the track. Every instruction that you give and all the rules that you make are met with resistance. When it seems impossible to steer them in the right direction and they are determined to pull at opposite ends from you, your heart breaks and all the while you are looking for a fix to the situation.

Many times when children are unwilling to listen to their parents, they are listening to their peers. Gaining the approval of friends seems much more important than living up to the standards that Mom and Dad have set for them. Motivated by pure love, parents set guidelines based on the best interest of the child, both in the present tense as well as the future. On the contrary, the only interest their peers have is fun for the moment. Sometimes adventures with their friends may find them in a mess that needs to be fixed. How painful it is when Mama can't fix it. Though they may fight against you and your rules, they are still looking to you to set boundaries.

Sadly, some Mother's children are led astray into a life of addiction to drugs, alcohol, or some other obsessive behavior, which holds them as a captured prisoner. Oh my, how they seem to always be searching for another fix. Instead of a temporary fix, leading to destruction and keeping them looking for the next fix, they need a permanent fix that gives true and lasting satisfaction. Mama's hopes and dreams for her young seemly have been flushed down the drain.

Mama aches and cries as she reaches out to help, but all help is rejected. Sleeplessness, tossing and turning, pondering and agonizing seem to fill Mama's nights, as she wonders how to fix her dearly beloved child. When daybreak comes, Mama goes about her daily duties with a weight sitting on her shoulder and a heavy heart. A child cannot destroy its own self without crushing Mama, because Mama's whole life is wrapped up in her family. When one of her young suffers, she endures the pain as well.

Mom, never give up and never loose sight of your hope. Deliverance has come to many, who were bound by addiction by the power of Jesus Christ. "If the Son therefore shall make you free, ye shall be free indeed." John 8:36 Both day and night, year after year a Mama cried and prayed for her son to be loosed and set free from addiction. She even headed up an army of prayer warriors to join forces with her as she fought for freedom for her dear son. Finally, one day her prayers were answered, as he was loosed from the bondage that once controlled him. When Mama couldn't fix him, she turned to the one who could. Jesus Christ gave him the real fix that he so desperately needed.

The Bible tells of a man who had two sons. The eldest son obeyed his father, staying by his side and working for him. But, the younger son asked his father to give him his portion of his inheritance. After the father granted him his request he gathered his inheritance and went and sowed his wild oats. Living the party lifestyle, he soon spent all that he had. Broke and in desperation, he returned unto his father. With welcoming arms and compassionate hugs and kisses, his father ran to meet him. Our heavenly Father meets His children in this same fashion. Mom, greet you son or daughter that has strayed from your teaching with this same compassion. Always be on the look out, expecting them to return back to the principles that you taught them.

Another issue facing this family was one of conflict between the two brothers. The brother who had stayed by his father's side, working hard and lived in obedience to the rules of the household, felt betrayed by the joyful reaction of his father, upon the return of his ruthless brother. The family in disarray, not living in harmony tugs at Mama's heartstrings, as well. Mama's dreams turn sour when squabbles arise within the family unit.

Mama, you were summoned to play referee when arguing broke out between your little tots. Pulling them apart, you made them settle their differences. Before long they were back to playing together again. Throughout the teenage years, Mama may still have needed to throw a little water on the fire from time to time. But once they have reached adulthood, Mama acting as referee may be perceived as Mama taking sides. Now Mama finds herself in a tougher position, trying to be peacemaker, while showing no partiality. Added your two cents worth into the pot just may be a big stick that stirs the flames into a much bigger fire. Facing Mom is a critical matter that needs to be handled very delicately and prayerfully. Days like this were never in your dreams.

Whether any of these issues affect your family or not, you can be certain that trying times will come and go throughout the course of life. Life will be in need of fixing from time to time. Not all of your dreams will come true. Some will be washed away like a wave washing the sand out from under your feet. Just when you think that you are standing on solid ground again, another storm is brewing, winds are howling, and the waves are crashing in. Hope will sometimes be hidden under a rubbish of despair. Digging away at the debris becomes a gruesome task. Continue digging until a ray of hope appears. The bright sunshine will eventually blossom from that little ray of hope.

While the other side of your dreams may have some days of gloom and doom, other days will have you running through beautiful, green fields of clover. Your imagination never showed you the beauty that your eyes now behold. Your dreams failed to conjure up the expression of love shown to you as your little tot, strolls in the house, eyes beaming with excitement, wearing a great big grin, and suddenly popping little hands out from the backside and with a little voice sweetly saying, "I picked you these flowers, Mommy". The happiness of that moment goes way beyond a dream.

Down the road of life, at times the love and kindness of your family will be more delightful than you thought possible. Little arms reaching up to you at the end of a long and tiring day are so refreshing. Weariness falls off of your shoulders as a little head finds a resting place, snuggled up against your face. No novel that you could read compares to reading a bedtime story to such an attentive audience with perked up little ears. Dreams never were this sweet.

This ride of Motherhood that you are on may bring you to a nice music or dance recital or possibly to a sporting event, maybe even a play of some sort. You smile and clap as one by one each child struts into the spotlight. But the smile turns into a big wide grin and the clap into a thunderous outburst as your youngster comes on the scene. Whatever the occasion, the best performer of the evening is riding home with you.

School days present challenges and disappointments along with achievements and rewards. You thought that your little one would be a model student until the teacher tells a different story. Some report card days may be met with a smile and others a frown. But on graduation day, you are thrilled to the bone regardless if you have an honor student or if that walk across the stage is by the skin of their teeth.

The accomplishments of your children throughout the years are dreams fulfilled for you. Their successes are your triumphs as well. On the other hand, their pain becomes your grief. In their victories you will soar with them. But their misfortunes will send a stabbing pain right through your heart. What needs to be fixed will have you always looking for a fix. But, when you can't find a fix, then look to The Master, who can fix what you can't.

Chapter Three

Watch the House

Oftentimes, dreams of the perfect world include a cute little house, surrounded by a white picket fence, and a good watchdog perched upon the porch. Sure the family dog is quite playful with Mom, Dad, and the children. Neighbors and friends who happen to drop by are met with a wagging tail and maybe even a lick on the hand. But, let some unwelcome intruder come along and playtime is over. With each snarl and growl, the white teeth are shining and the eyes are glaring, as the defense mechanism kicks in. Set and ready to defend his territory, this old dog may ward off an intrusion by sending the uninvited guest in a run. The whole neighborhood may be alerted that danger lies within the wings by the barking of this family dog.

Mom, your prayers may become like a watchdog, alerting you of the sounds of danger, moving in for an attack upon your family. Just like the dog that has done his duty, your prayers will serve their purpose, as well. For instance, I recall a certain morning that as I was earnestly in prayer, I felt a sense of urgency to pray for protection upon my family. As the events of the day unfolded, my daughter was involved in a minor collision. The passenger door of her car was t-boned by another car. My darling granddaughter would have been sitting in that seat, except that she suddenly changed her mind at the last moment and decided to stay home with her Dad. Oh, by the way, this daughter was pregnant with another beautiful grandchild of mine. No one was hurt, not a minor scrape or bruise was found. During prayer time that morning, in a solitude moment, being secluded in the presence of God, sounding waves shouted **Danger!** As I interceded to God, asking for His protection upon all of my family, a sense of peace swept over me. To some, Mother's intuition would be the label applied to such an experience. However, this was nothing less than divine discernment from my heavenly Father, and divine intervention. Thankfully on that day, I was watching the house. All the fury of danger was met head on by a praying Mom.

While the family may be hearing the sounds of alarm from the ever so watchful guard dog, a powerful message is also being sent to the predator. The prey will not be so easily taken. Perpetrators hear the signal of danger zone ahead at the sound of the old barking dog. Mom, your heartfelt, sincere prayers become an alarming sound in the ears of the enemy, as he moves in for an all out assault on your family. As Satan, the roaring lion viciously attacks; your prayers will be an even more vicious attack against him. Standing in the face of the enemy, the growling and howling of your prayers will announce to him that he has met a force greater than he. "Greater is he that is in you, than he that is in the world." 1 John 4:4

Although, Satan may not back down, he knows that he has a fight on his hands. He is familiar with the authority that is in the name of Jesus. That authority had stood up to him, slapped him, beat him and defeated him time and time again. "When the enemy shall come in like a flood, the spirit of the Lord shall lift up a standard against him." Isaiah 59:19 When the enemy embarks upon the standard that the Lord has raised, he becomes the defeated foe. As the flag of defeat is waved before the enemy, you are waving a banner of victory. He has no weapons that cannot be destroyed by your powerful weapon, called prayer. "No weapon that is formed against thee shall prosper." Isaiah 54:17 Mom, stand your ground, set a ever so prayerful watch, and defend your territory.

Countless number of times circumstances have been changed in the life of a child, all because of the prayers of Mama. An adult daughter was having difficulties with her job due to a very moody boss. Now Mama couldn't go to her daughter's workplace and fix it, but Mama could pray. Instead of praying for the boss to be fired, she simply prayed for God to intervene and work this situation out. Shortly after Mom began praying for this matter, the boss applied for a different position within the company. Soon this grumpy boss was exploring new horizons, and the daughter's load was made much lighter. God had answered a prayer and things became more pleasant for both parties involved.

Praying for this boss to join the unemployment line would have been a prayer prayed with the wrong attitude and a very selfish motive. However, praying for God to bless both of them was very appropriate and very powerful. When God commanded that we pray for our enemies, he instructed that we bless them and not curse them. "But I say unto you, Love your enemies, bless them that curse you, do good to them that hate you, and pray for them which despitefully use you, and persecute you." Matthew 5:44

The unrelenting yelping of Mama's prayers has diminished illnesses and diseases. High fevers have succumbed to the prayers of Mama. Babies have been born with infirmities that from a natural medical prognosis were to suffer ill effects all the days of their life. But, prayer became the cure. At a young age, my own daughter was diagnosed with a heart condition, known as, mitral valve prolapse. Having all the symptoms and through medical testing, our family doctor confirmed her illness. He also stated that there was no cure and that she would be on medication for the rest of her life. Trust me, it didn't take many episodes of shortness of breath and pain in the chest, to drive this Mama to her knees. I am very happy to say, that she has been off of all medication and has had no occurrence of this illness in over ten years.

However, not all ailments are cured according to Mama's choosing. A child living a lifetime of affliction does not indicate that Mama did not carefully watch over and blanket her young with prayer. Several years ago, born unto a faithful minister and his wonderful wife was a precious little baby, who was diagnosed with cystic fibrosis. This family has been on a wild roller coaster ride ever since. They have prayed and sought the prayers of others. In spite of their prayers, they have experienced many highs and lows throughout the years. As they asked for healing, they were given courage, and in their weaknesses, the grace of God has strengthened them. "My grace is sufficient for thee: for my strength is made perfect in weakness." 2 Corinthians 12:9

Seeking after God, they have seen his hand pull them through one storm after another. The Holy Spirit has caressed this Mom through many nights, as she slept in a hospital room next to the bedside of her little angel. No doubt the severity of the attacks upon this child's body has been lessen many times as the result of the sincere prayers that have been lifted up unto the heavenly Father on her behalf. While these parents would have chosen an instant miraculous healing, God chose to show them many miracles all along the way. Nonetheless, prayer has meticulously watched over this adorable child.

Aside from health concerns, various other trials will surely race down your trail of life, meeting you head on. Hiding underneath the bushes, an arsenal of explosives may be well concealed, lying in wait for an attack upon your family. But, like a bloodhound, your prayers will sniff them out. Then, the howling of your cries unto the Lord will snuff them out. As surely as troubles will face your family, you can count upon God to miraculously show his face, and his hand to calm the troubled waters.

Financial woes certainly have caused a few ripples in the water for many families. Oh, the stories that could be told of provision that has been met as a result of a praying Mom. A certain widow lady, with little mouths to feed, many times did not know where the next meal would come from, yet her children never went lacking. As she prayed and trusted in God, food would always be supplied from one meal to the next. How thankful she was to God, that she never had to tuck her children in bed at nighttime with a hungry stomach. The powerful prayers of this praying Mother overpowered the sting of poverty.

Another lady friend of mine was continually in prayer concerning her husband's working hours, which had been drastically cut. Of course, as the hours were cut, so was the family income. In her own words, she was totally amazed how God provided the needs of the family during this time. Before long, instead of asking God to give him more work, she was praying for God to strengthen him to do all the work that was set before him. You see, his work schedule changed from two or possibly three days a week, to six days a week. Struck down by prayer, lack fell by the wayside, and provision prevailed.

Another huge dagger into Mama's heart is when her sweet and innocent children turn rebellious, wandering so far away from her teachings and the life that she so carefully exemplified to them. With the young buck and the sassy little doe kicking their heels high into the air, broken-hearted Mama is sitting at home, with tears streaming down her face. But, as Mama turns those tears of sadness into cries unto the Lord, hopelessness falls by the wayside. With renewed strength, she vows to fight until the bitter end, using her only weapon called prayer. This is a fight to be fought in the spiritual realm rather than fighting with the unruly rebel. Many prodigals have humbly come back home on the wings of Mama's prayers. When rebellion came face to face with the prayers of a praying Mom, prayed in the authority of Jesus name, rebellion then met a force greater that itself. Defiance was crushed and chewed up like a bone in a dog's mouth.

During those awful times that your children wandered aimlessly, so far away from the training that you so diligently taught them, Mama's prayers so carefully watched over them, by dispatching angels to protect them from many dangers. Many pitfalls that they could have fallen into, but those prayers prevented their feet from sliding in. How wonderful to have the promises of God to cling to during such trying times. "Train up a child in the way he should go: and when he is old, he will not depart from it." Proverbs 22:6 How soothing to know that buried deep within their heart lies your teachings that they cannot escape from. Mama, this is a promise from God that you can rely upon.

Many years ago a young man strayed away from his godly training. As he sewed his wild oats, Mama never stopped praying. Constantly searching his heart was the word of God, which had been deeply planted and rooted within his spirit. The prayers of his dear Mama watched over his every step. Those prayers safely guided him out of darkness and back onto the lighted path that shone ever so brightly before him. As the Holy Spirit beckoned, he answered the call that pulled on his heartstrings. Becoming an ordained minister of the gospel of Jesus Christ, he became an instrument, which the Holy Spirit used to lead many others onto the path of righteousness. The watchful eye that was sparked by Mama's prayers never lost sight of this young man during his wondering years. His ministering years were also well covered by the prayers of Mama.

Like most families, oftentimes you have probably been attacked by a whirlwind of confusion. Racing through your mind are nothing but questions and no answers to be found. Then suddenly, riding in on the hem of Mama's prayers many wise decisions has come. Frazzled and wrecked nerves have a way of distorting a sound mind. Seemly your whole family is unraveling at the seams, not knowing which way to turn, the road ahead seems to be clouded over with a clump of mud. Crawling out from beneath the murky waters, Mama begins seeking direction and guidance from the Lord. Then all at once wisdom comes knocking on your heart's door. As a good solid resolution is unveiled right before your eyes, the uncertainly of it all begins to dissipate. "If any of you lack wisdom, let him ask of God, that giveth to all men liberally, and upbraideth not; and it shall be given him." James 1:5 Instead of wandering around in a state of confusion, ask God for wisdom. As you watch over your house, prayerfully consider all decisions that you must make.

Much like plugging a lamb into an electrical outlet, flipping the switch, and there is light, those prayers are connecting you with an ever powerful guiding light called the Holy Spirit, whose eyesight has no obstructions. Through spiritual eyes you now may see things that you never saw in the natural realm. Dancing all around you may be red flags waving you away from danger. But, in the midst of all the flags you may see a straight and narrow path leading to safety.

Worse than wallowing in your own confused state of mind, is seeing your child swallowed up in a sea of bewilderment. Tangled up in a bundle of seaweed, life has been squeezed out of their thought processing, obscuring their judgment. Swimming upstream against the current, life becomes a struggle. But, the prayers of Mama can ever so gently untangle the mess one piece at a time. Just like seeing the forest through the trees, they begin to see a clear path around the obstacles. Mama, your prayers attacked that sea of confusion and perplexity with the force of a wild ferocious attack dog.

The enemy lurks from all angles, coming forth as a wolf disguised in sheep's clothing. His deceptive practices, he will try to conceal. He will come along beside you with a smile on his face, joining together with your family pretending to be a friend, when all the while he is a foe. "For Satan himself is transformed into an angel of light." 2 Corinthians 11:14 The word transformed in this text refers to putting on a mask, faking his darkness as light. Using deceptive devices his objective is to trample over you with every turn in the road. He is ever looking for ways to oppress you. Allow him free reign and he will move you from oppression to depression.

Be on alert at all times! Keep your ears perked and your eyes searching all around the house, even when you are perched upon the porch chewing on a bone, because never will there be a time when it is safe to let your guard down. If you have a watchdog guarding over your home, would there be days that you just decided that you didn't need the services of the dear old pooch? Well, that just may be the day that your home becomes invaded. Likewise, there are no days when prayer is not needed, and there are no occasions when the Lord is not attentive to the prayers of his children.

As the Jews worked, rebuilding the walls around Jerusalem, for the walls had been destroyed; their enemies had a conspiracy against them and tried to hinder their work. But, they called on God and set a watch against the enemy. "Nevertheless we made our prayer unto our God, and set a watch against them day and night, because of them." Nehemiah 4:9 Notice, not a day or night went by without the watchmen being on duty. Just as Satan so cleverly tries to join forces with his opposition, so did the enemies of these hard working Jews. "And our adversaries said, they shall not know, neither see, till we come in the midst among them, and slay them, and cause the work to cease." Nehemiah 4:11 The remainder of this chapter shows the laborers at work with their weapons at their side until the work was completed. Mama, just like these Jews, never will there be a time to set aside your watch and the safeguarding of your family.

You may go about your daily chores with the weapon of PRAYER strapped across your shoulder. While you cook and clean, you may call on Jesus, asking Him to cover your household underneath his sheltering wing. While your wingspan can only go so far, his is unlimited. While you do laundry, you may lean upon Jesus to look after your little ones. As you fold the clothes that those little tots will wear, you may bless them with a gentle little prayer. Seeking the Lord while doing the scrubbing produces more than shining floors, sparkling glass, and a clean toilet. How comforting to know that while off to work you go, Jesus is watching over your family. When it comes time to lay your head down at night, you may rest peacefully in the hand of the Almighty God, knowing that He has dispatched angels over your home.

"For he shall give his angels charge over thee,
to keep thee in all thy ways." Psalm 91:11.

Deeply and compassionately, the heavenly Father is concerned about the needs of your family and the deepest desires of your heart. But, genuine prayer runs much deeper than presenting Him with your needs. Prayer is an avenue where upon a love relationship is built with the creator. As your love for Him deepens, He shines a little brighter, and your list of needs becomes a little dimmer. Just as enjoying a meal will strengthen the body; time spent with the Lord will nourish your soul. The bond of love experienced between you and God will grow increasingly stronger through your prayer time. Out of your love for Him, praise should lovingly flow from the bottom of your heart. Gracing your lips will be words of adoration unto the King of Kings and Lord of Lords. Reflecting upon his goodness and the magnitude of his greatness will fill your heart with gratitude. Then with thanksgiving, bring your needs unto Him.

When singing in the shower becomes praising in the shower, soap and water, dirt and grime is not all that goes down the drain. Vocalizing a good old hymn or a chorus of praise also washes away your blues. Lifting up praise unto the Lord will lift the spirit of your burdened soul. As your heaviness is lifted, your faith becomes stronger. Suddenly, hope is restored and strength renewed. On the heels of jubilant praise and adoration to God, comes a whispered prayer of thanksgiving, knowing that He is fully capable of handling any situation that arises. Your focus has now shifted from the problem to the problem solver. Suddenly, that shower has become much more refreshing. While lathering your body with soap and shampooing your hair, your soul has been revived. Much like an old dog that once with a snarling growl had its hair raised on its back, but now is settled back on the porch wagging its tail.

Through prayer, you have a golden opportunity to ask God's blessing upon your family. The Lord gave instruction to Moses and Aaron to bless the children of Israel with the words of the following prayer. How fitting and appropriate for parents to pray this same prayer over their children.

> "The Lord bless Thee and keep Thee
> The Lord make his face to shine upon Thee
> And be gracious unto Thee
> The Lord lift up his countenance upon Thee
> And give thee peace."
>
> Numbers 6:24-26

On occasion, during my own personal prayer time, I have turned to these verses and asked this blessing upon my husband, each child, each grandchild, and son-in-law that makes up my family. Mom, please pause for a bit of time, insert the name of each family member, as you recite this prayer of blessing over each individual member of your family. You have just pronounced God's blessing into the life of your children. How can they live anything less than a blessed life? Asking God to bless them and keep them in his care sets a watch over your young, way beyond what your eyes could ever behold. In the reflection of all of His tender mercy and grace, as they behold His face, ever so gently He will shine upon them. He will stand up and give His attention to every little detail of their being. They may always rest in His peace. A blessed life does not ensure that each breath will be filled with happiness, or that each day will bring in an abundance of wealth. The blessings of God run much deeper than circumstances. But, joy and peace can still be found at any time and through any situation.

There is never a time like the present to begin praying for each child. As that wonderful little embryo is snuggled nice and warm inside of your womb, ask God to watch over and protect it, birthing it safely into this world. Pray God's Blessing upon this child, while asking for His perfect plan to be fulfilled throughout all of its life.

Equally important, never is it too late to begin watching over your children with your prayers. For that Mom whose children have a few years of age on them and you have never covered them in your prayers, now is the time to begin. Unleash that watchdog and watch the Holy Spirit hover over them. Now is the time to sound the alarm, watchdog on guard.

Never too early, never too late, and never give up! Keep up the watch and stay in the fight until your dying day. Do not be overtaken by discouragement, rather run into the sheltering arms of your heavenly Father, who is ready to strengthen and encourage you. Try taking a bone out of the mouth of a big brutish dog.

You will find that the old hound does not become discouraged and sheepishly walk away. That old dog is ready for a fight. Your loved ones are worth the time that you invest in watching over them through your prayers, declaring to the enemy that they will not be snatched out of the palm of God's hand. Many times some sweet dear Mother has prayed until her hairs turn gray without seeing the results of her prayers. But then, during her ripe golden years, the fruit of her labors began to blossom.

Mom, one-day life comes to a dead end. Taking your final breath will not take the life out of your prayers. Your prayers have safely guarded your young. Many times, divine wisdom has guided them through the course of life, thanks to your prayers. Tables have turned in an instant, as you bowed your head, or your knees hit the floor. The power of those prayers will long outlive you. "Thy prayers and thine alms are come up for a memorial before God." Acts 10:4 Your prayers will never cease to come up before God. With each prayer, you have set a watch over your loved ones. You have sounded the alarm, unleashed an arsenal of weapons, warring the enemy away from you home. When time comes for you to be laid to rest, your prayers will still act as a watchdog caring for your loved ones, seeing them all the way to the end of their life.

Unknown are the times that harm has been kept at bay, because of Mama's prayers. Much brokenness that Mama could not fix, but as you prayed you witnessed a transformation take place. The malicious barking of Mama's prayers has crushed walls that seemly held your young hostage. Sometimes that wall collapsed and tumbled down in an instant. At others times the wall was chiseled down one prayer at a time. Regardless of the timing or the method the wall crumbled, setting the captive free.

Yes, Mama your prayers are like a good old watchdog, set in motion, ready to defend when the enemy moves in. Take your stand, watch over your family, and pray with the same aggressiveness and authority of a vicious attack dog. The sounds of danger may be beyond the listening ears of the old hound dog, lying on the front porch, or running through the yard. But, distance sets no boundaries of your prayers into the listening ears of your heavenly Father. You may not be able to fix everything, but you can always set a prayerful watch over your family. In all that you do, do not neglect to watch the house.

Chapter Four

Hold Onto Your Faith

Dangling high above sinking sand, barely hanging on, clinging to a rope with a tight grip becomes the only lifeline to stay afloat. When trouble comes rushing in like a mighty rushing wave, faith will be the lifeline that keeps you planted firmly on solid ground. No matter how high the storm rages, the waters cannot cover your head and your feet cannot be pulled down by the under current. Yes, faith in The Almighty God will keep you floating on top of every trial thrown your way.

As faith looks beyond the visible and sees the invisible, it clings to a knowledge that is unseen and unexplainable. Expectancy fills the atmosphere as you call upon the name of the Lord. Instead of wondering if God will move, faith looks for the moving of His hand. Firmly fixed in your spiritual vision is evidence that cannot be touched by the hand or seen through your physical eye. Logical reasoning may take the breath right out of you, knocking you to your knees. But, holding onto your faith will keep you strolling in green pastures.

Reaching way beyond the scope of merely believing, faith moves into the realm of wholeheartedly trusting. Trust not only believes that God is Almighty, and knows that God can do all things. But, understands that God, in all of His wisdom truly knows what is best and how to achieve the best results. Trusting God means holding onto your faith, letting go of your worries, and giving the reins over to Him.

Faith moves forward, not looking back upon the devastating blows of the past, nor the present raging storm, but lunges into the future with a bright hope. Exuberant anticipation of what is to be instead of dwelling on what has been. Yesterday's fears and the disappointments and failures of the past will fade ever so dimly, as you march onward, expecting great days ahead. Faith allows you to see through the dark clouds and visualize the bright sunshine shining ever so brightly over the horizon.

As the highs and lows of life come along the way, faith smoothes out the rocky road. Confidently you may drudge through today's valley, knowing that its path may lead you high upon a mountaintop tomorrow. Faith keeps you climbing that mountain instead of being swallowed up in a cave down in the valley. The deep, dark, hard times of life may be dreary, but also is very fertile soil for faith to grow and become stronger. Often times in the valley, people learn to become God-dependent and not self-reliant.

Faith must be a lifestyle; otherwise it will be here today and gone tomorrow. Faith that wavers back and forth with seesawing circumstances will have your head spinning and your stomach queasy as you struggle to keep yourself afloat, and all the while you just keep sinking. You cannot live day to day in faith until you understand that faith does not hinge on what God does or does not do, but is firmly fixed on who He is. Situations will change, but God is a constant God who never changes. "Jesus Christ the same yesterday, and today and for ever." Hebrews 13:8 His love is unending, with mercies that are new every morning and

His kingdom is everlasting. How could you lose faith in God when He has not lost His power and authority?

Wandering thoughts that lead to questions such as why, how and what if, is a gateway to doubt. Unresolved doubt opens the door to fear. Fear is like a hatchet, hacking and cutting through the very core of your faith. Suddenly, an unending triangle is formed. The bigger the fear is, the more doubts will come, leading to even more uncontrolled mind games. The drifting mind will play this game over and over again. Take control of your thoughts before doubt and fear takes control of you. "Casting down imaginations, and every high thing that exalteth itself against the knowledge of God, and bringing into captivity every thought to the obedience of Christ." 2 Corinthians 10:5 Cast aside every thought that leads to doubting before fear raises a force against the very faith within you.

Fear sees nothing but obstacles, leaving you paralyzed, afraid to move forward. On the other hand, faith sees the hand of God pushing and shoving, destroying every obstacle that is standing in your path. Fear destroys your faith, leaving you discouraged and defeated. Faith destroys fear, bringing peace, joy and victory into your life. Fear says there is no way, while faith knows that God is the way. Fear darkens the path that God has so perfectly designed for you, swallowing you up into a pile of confusion. Faith shines a spotlight for you to follow, directing your every step. Every hard trial of life presents an opportunity to learn valuable lessons, turn your weaknesses into strengths, build your character and enhance your relationship with God.

Faith opens the door of opportunity while fear slams the door shut.

Faith in the sovereignty of God is your defense against doubt and fear. Before you go spirally down into a well of hopelessness, combat those wayward thoughts by standing upon His promises, knowing that He has the authority to back up every word that He has spoken. "Above all, taking the shield of faith, wherewith ye shall be able to quench all the fiery darts of the wicked." Ephesians 6:16   Faith is your shield of protection against a doubting mind, turning uncertainties into a calm assurance, an absolute knowing within your spirit that God is still God and in control.   Instead of allowing your faith to be dismantled by fear, boldly stand in the face of fear itself, courageously speaking words of faith, then your faith will calmly dispel fear.

A few years ago an accident struck down a daughter of a believing Mama.   Unable to speak, the only communication with this beautiful loved one has been the blinking of an eye or wiggling a toe upon command. No getting out of bed and taking a walk, not even a few steps, she has laid bedridden for all of this time. Being fed by a feeding tube, not even a bite of food has touched her lips since the date of the accident. But, fear has not been an enemy to this Mama, because her faith is greater than the uncertainty of if all. The foundation of her faith is built upon her unwavering trust in the Lord, not based upon her understanding of the matter at hand. Overpowering her heartache is her hope in Jesus Christ. Bedded deep within her heart is a love and commitment for the

Lord, which far exceeds the circumstance facing her. Lovingly she has been at her child's bedside day after day for months on end, and then the months turned into years. Dedicated as she has been, to care for her precious daughter, her strong dedication unto the Lord has remained just as true and steadfast.

This is not a Mama new to faith in the Lord. She has been walking in faith with assured confidence in God for over a half of century. But, her faith has still been tested and tried. She has truly passed the test with flying colors. Without question her trust in God is still as strong as ever. Trying her faith were difficulties harder than she had ever imagined. But by God's grace, her faith has shined as pure gold once more.

She continues holding onto hope that this child will rise up off her of bed of affliction, longing for the day that she will walk and talk, laugh and sing again. Seeing her child to live again in some normalcy of life is ever in her heart and prayers. Mama knows that this daughter joining the family around the table for a holiday celebration once more is not impossible. "for with God all things are possible." Mark 10:27 Delightful it would be to stand next to her, singing songs of praise in a Sunday church service again.

However, she well knows that should that not become a reality in this life, that those things she will witness again. She will see her dancing on a street paved with gold, magnificently glittering in all its beauty. Her voice will be mingled with countless others in a beautiful, heavenly choir, ringing out praises, songs of sweet hallelujahs around the throne of God. She will dine with her again at the "Marriage Supper of The Lamb." Regardless of what happens on this earth, Mama's hope will not be overshadowed, her faith in Jesus Christ will never fade. As Mama has held onto her faith in God, her faith has securely held Mama together.

Walking by faith one day at a time, one experience at a time, through the good times and bad, would certainly define the walk of a sister-in-law of mine. Cerebral Palsy was the fate of my little nephew, Joshua, who came into our family fifteen years ago. His Mama has diligently met the challenging needs of her precious little boy every step of the way. Many years she spent chauffeuring him to physical, occupation, and speech therapies, along with numerous Doctor Appointments. And by the way, some of the Doctor visits have been met with encouraging news, but some with very despairing news. But Mama's faith challenged every bad report with the report of the Lord. She steadfastly refused to believe anything other than, what was impossible through medical science, was totally possible through God. By faith she released all of her worries and cares concerning little Joshua unto the Lord.

As a newborn baby, the medical prognosis of Joshua was anything but good. According to scientific knowledge he would never take a step, or crawl across the floor, never speak a word, not even would a smile ever cross his face. Mama would listen to the medical report with her natural ears, and then through her spiritual eyes, she would visualize him walking and talking. Mama knew that her little Joshua would become all that God wanted him to be. Knowing that

God would either heal his condition or give the grace and strength to her and her husband to care for him was her solace.

In his early days, his Mother would keep the television tuned to Christian programs. His attention was drawn to the television, as certain ministers would appear on the screen. As they would began to pray for healing, Joshua, who was not to ever crawl, would hurriedly scoot himself across the floor, reaching his little hands up, touching the television screen. As a very young child, he knew that he needed a miracle from God.

Now any parent may be thrilled with the first few steps of their little tot, but one can only imagine the excitement with Joshua's first steps. Although, his came with the use of a walker, each step brought overflowing joy into Mama's heart, along with all the rest of the family. He still walks with the aid of a walker, but Praise God he is still walking. For years he used a wheelchair at school, but recently stopped taking the wheelchair, and motivates himself around school all day on his walker. Praise the Lord!

Carrying on a conversation is not on the same level as most people. But sheer joy welled up within the entire family as words began to come out of his little mouth. And as words turned into sentences the excitement grew, and so did Mama's faith. Like other children, Joshua repeats words that he hears, and sometime they may not be nice. Mama brings correction while other family members giggle underneath their breath. Even though his verbal communication is on a small child's level, each word is nothing short of miraculous.

You should see the smile that supposedly would never be. A grin that goes from ear to ear with nothing but white teeth shining in between is a sight to behold. Tickling the ear of all who hear is the laughter coming from deep within and can be heard throughout an entire neighborhood. His laugh is quite contagious. One good round of laughter coming from Joshua could wipe the frown off of the biggest grouch around. And even in the saddest moments, the joy of hearing his laughter would lighten anyone's heart.

The proclamation from a neurosurgeon that he would never have any cognitive skills was denounced quite early. One particular Sunday, I volunteered to stay home from church and keep him, allowing his Mother to attend service, since she had missed several weeks, attending to his needs. His condition had not allowed her to have him out in public for quite some time. He became anxious to see his Mom. Looking at the front door, he called her several times. Each time I would calmly assure him that Mama was at church and would come back as soon as church was over. Finally, after several times, he bowed his little head and said "Amen, Come Mom." At two years of age, he knew that church ended with an Amen. The Lord reported that he could do what had previously been stated that he could not do.

Fifteen years have come and gone, and each new day is still a challenge. But, Mama is still holding onto her faith, and faith is still holding Mama up. Relying upon the Lord for strength, Mama lifts and pulls her son up, all one hundred thirty-five pounds on a daily basis. Swimming is his basic means of exercise. Getting him down the steps into the pool and then pulling him back up had become a hard struggle. Mama prayed and trusted that the Lord would help with this issue. One day a man stopped by and asked if they were interested in getting a lift to let him down and bring him back up out of the pool. Emphatically yes, Mama replied, but they could not afford one. This man knew of an organization that donated such equipment to those who need it. Soon the lift was installed into their pool at no cost to them. Faith had proven to work again.

Amazingly faith brought this child into this family. By faith Mom and Dad adopted this little baby, knowing all of the facts concerning his medical condition and the many challenges that would be facing them. Both Mom and Dad acted upon faith, not facts. Both knew full well that God could either change the facts or give them the strength to face the challenge. Another couple had planned to adopt Joshua from birth, but decided against going through with the adoption plans because of the physical ailments that accompanied him. But, Joshua's parents knew that he needed someone to care for him, and by faith they accepted the challenge and brought this wonderful baby into their family, who has been a blessing not only to his parents and siblings, but to all the extended family as well.

Looking though a museum of those who have lived by faith, you would find a big statue of Noah. Following the Word of God and the leading of the Holy Spirit, he built the ark when it made no sense to anyone else. Raindrops were not falling on his head when he began building. But, by faith he could see the flood that was to come, only because God had spoken it. He refused to be persuaded by the opposition and he obeyed God. Because of Noah's obedience, he and his family were safe. While God desired to spare Noah and his family from the destruction of the flood, He did not build the ark for him. Noah had to gather the wood, go to work, and build.

Mama you are in the same boat as Noah was. The safety of his family depended upon his obedience to the Lord and his willingness to build the ark. Noah's faith was more than just believing that God would spare his family. He had to put action behind his faith. God has instructed you to teach your children the commands of the Lord. Each time you teach them God's word, carry them to church, and set a godly example to them, you are leading your children into the safety of the Ark. You may sometimes need to teach by way of discipline. A lack of discipline may open the door of the ark and allow danger to come in. Oftentimes your children will find that your ways are not nearly as popular as what everyone else is doing. You must be like Noah, stand firm upon your faith and follow the instructions of the Lord and not the folly of the crowd.

Faith is too good to keep to yourself, pass it on! Of course you cannot open the heart of another person and pour faith into them. But, others can learn to depend upon God by watching a good role model. Mama in all the different ways that you are a pattern for your children to live by, none will be more important than living a life of faith. Watching Mama hold onto her faith and weather whatever storm comes her way proves beneficial for generations to come.

For instance, a young man was involved in a tragic accident, a couple of years ago. Initially, he spent months in the hospital, sent home only to return back and forth to the hospital like a revolving door. Scans and test he has had by the score. His body is still broken and battered, needing twenty-four hour care. His Mama has held onto her faith, because her Mama taught her to always trust and believe in the Lord. Even his sister has stood by in faith because as a child she witnessed the faith of not only Mama, but Grandma as well. From generation to generation, faith was passed on through teaching and by example.

Mama, whatever dilemma you are facing, refuse to listen to the discouraging and negative voices that come along. Job was one who turned a deaf ear to any naysayer who happened by, when his world fell completely apart. When the day of Job's calamity had ended, all that he had left standing was a nagging wife and three disgruntled friends. All his worldly possessions were destroyed, and death had taken all of his children. But, nothing could destroy his faith. One by one, each of his friends came comforting Job with these words "curse God and die." Adding insult to injury, instead of standing by her husband, his wife chummed right in with the discouraging friends. Nonetheless, Job held onto his faith and the end of Job's life was more blessed that the beginning.

Giving up on your faith is way too costly. You simply cannot afford to be swayed by anyone or any circumstance to lose faith and wonder into a pit of hopelessness. More will be lost than just your courage. Pivoting upon your faith will be consequences

61

impacting you and your family. While faith does not make God capable, neither does unbelief make him unable, He does respond to faith. Jesus did not do very many miracles in His own village because of their unbelief. Not because that He was deemed powerless, but because that He did not overstep the boundary lines that they had drawn.

While God does answer prayer and grants desires to His children, do not mistake faith as simply handing over to God some wish list to be fulfilled. Trusting Him to revise the list, fitting you into His plan instead of demanding that your own plans come together is faith. Even when you don't understand the steps that He has ordered for you, by faith, you will walk them anyway, because faith is not founded on understanding. As a Mama, you will not always understand the happenings of your family. Quite frankly, your wish list probably will not always come together according to your specifications. Ask your heavenly Father to design the list and trust Him.

While everyone may encounter a few hard pills to swallow, some people face much harder issues in life than others. Try as hard as you may, and you simply cannot find a fix. Faith recognizes that although you cannot fix it, you know who can. But, taken a step further, faith also accepts His fix, even when it appears much different than what you were expecting. By faith, gather all of the broken pieces of your family, and offer them up to God, asking Him to do as He chooses. Polished and fine are the treasures that He will make of your brokenness, much more costly than those of your dreams.

Chapter Five

Connect the Dots

Connect the dots, a process whereby pictures are created. The image of the picture is concealed until all the lines have been drawn from dot to dot and so forth. Knowing the image the picture is to portray, an artist places dots all along the surface. Before one dot is placed upon the artwork, the designer must have a final picture in view. Once all the dots are connected, an outline of the image is revealed. Completing the picture will be an array of various colors painted between the lines.

You did not just blow in on the canvas of time, like a leaf being aimless blown by the wind. The master artist fit you into the scene, with an ordained purpose and designed plan in place for you. "For I know the thoughts that I think toward you, saith the Lord, thoughts of peace, and not of evil, to give you an expected end." Jeremiah 29:11 Like an artist placing dots upon an artistic canvas, the heavenly Father has already placed dots along your path. A life of peace and a future of hope are in His plans for you.

Navigating you through the course of life, which by the way seems to be an obstacle course, He will methodically lead you from dot to dot unveiling a piece of artwork unmatched by any artist. Numerous circumstances of all different shapes and sizes pave the road of life. Each situation is only a small little dot of time compared to the scope of all eternity. Life as you now live in your earthen vessel is only temporary, but must be lived with an eternal perspective, because it has an eternal purpose. Placing all the dots that outline your path, eternity was the final picture that the Father had in mind.

A sheer delight will be some dots, captivating you with love, peace, contentment, joy and happiness. Looking up into the sky, the twinkling stars catch your eye with their dazzling beauty. The sound of laughter ringing in your ears is as the sound of joyful music. At other times a sweet, soft melody is beautifully played upon the strings of your heart. The thrill of the moment has you bubbling over with excitement, living in ecstasy. Though, you would love to stay frozen in that moment of time, the journey of life moves you on to the next dot.

Sometimes the next little speck of time will be unpleasant. Many dotted areas will be composed of hardships, trying your patience, testing your durability, and building your character. Your heart that once was filled with lovely music now aches as it is ripped and torn apart. Confused by circumstances that you do not understand, you wonder what lies ahead. Where will the next dot lead you? Knowing where each dot is leading you is not important. But, knowing who is leading you is of the essence. Know the one with the paintbrush in His hand. Trust in His plan because He knows best. With the final picture in sight, He placed all the dots mapping out your path.

Many happenings of life are nothing more than a dot, uniquely placed on your painting canvas for a particular season and specific purpose. Some dots may come into play simply because you tried to side step the next dot on the canvas. Instead of connecting, you disconnect, running circles around your next appointed destination. This results in the creation of a brand new dot, standing in the way of the picture being completed as God intended, according to His perfect plan. Using some course sandpaper, much harsh rubbing may be necessary to erase the damage and smooth out the edges, as the charted course of life continues.

Of Course, the evil one, Satan himself will certainly plant some thorns and thistles, camouflaged as God's little dots, along the way. Stay alert and be aware at all times, else your vision will become impaired and blurred, causing confusion between the dots and the thorns. Oftentimes evil will be disguised as good, and good may be disguised as evil. The sly old deceiver's tricks will never take the Father blindsided. He already has the dots deciphered from the thorns. Assuredly, the heavenly Father knows just how to meticulously maneuver you around each thorny bush. Unlike your human nature, God will never be fooled. The completed portrait is ever before His perfect eyes.

Encountering an unpleasant dot in time, or worse yet, being pricked by an ugly old thorn may be painful, and possibly arouse a few emotions that you would rather keep a lid on. You may choose to become like the Israelites, by moaning and groaning all the way through, or you could have your feathers ruffled and spout off your mouth like Peter did on occasions. Another option would be following the example of Job, waiting patiently upon the Lord, or you could sing praises like Paul and Silas did while imprisoned. Your response may determine whether you grow or stumble and falter.

How long that you must ride a bumpy ride or be jammed into a tight squeeze may be determined by your attitude. Your cooperation as He steers you through the course of life will be most helpful. Resistance or downright rebellion may keep you bound up for a little while longer. By no means, am I suggesting that full cooperation will prevent you from ever encountering a painful time of life. But, a wrong attitude can prevent you from learning, developing, and maturing, henceforth, holding up the process of moving to the next stage of life. As problems arise throughout life, lying before you is a golden opportunity to allow your faith to grow stronger. Do not use this as an opportune time to whine, complain, and pout like the Israelites did, causing them to wander in the wilderness for forty years.

You may take it all in stride as you are met by an unpleasant dot, testing your patience with challenging circumstances. Courageously you march on, never missing a drumbeat. The pricking of a painful thorn may even cause your endurance level to rise up a few notches as you get up and brush yourself off. Quietly and gently you may continue on without ever uttering a groan.

On the other hand, when your children get hung up on that same thorn bush or uncomfortable dot in time, a whole new indignation rises up within Mama. You are now ready to go to war. The battle just got heated up a few more degrees. Ruffling up Mama Hen's feathers is one thing, and quite another to mess with Mama's little chickens. The suffering of your children will send you frantically searching for a quick fix as agony grips and rips your heart. You may go into a frenzy panic mode, causing much anxiety and unsettledness to rise up within you. Desperately Mama wants to fix it, but sometimes Mama can't. But, the heavenly Father knows how to rearrange the muddled mess, and point them in the direction of the next set of dots on their canvas of life.

Most likely not all of your prayers will be answered in the same fashion as you prayed. Figuring it all out, maybe you pray earnestly for your plan to come together according to your terms. All you need God to do is to listen and follow your instructions as you tell Him what to do, how to do, and when to do, and problem will be solved. Unfortunately, many Christians have sometimes prayed with that kind of attitude, which is a prayer led from a heart of self-sufficiency, instead of relying on God. Quite frankly, that is much like trying to place the dots and take the paintbrush into your own hands and then wonder why God is not moving. The paint will brush on much smoother by joining God in his plans rather than expecting Him to bless yours. Consult the creator of the painting before drawing new lines on the surface. Ask Him to lead you to the next dot, instead of creating you own. Avoid placing a big smudge mark on your canvas by seeking for godly wisdom and guidance in everything that you do. By the way Mama, be careful not to place unnecessary dots and draw new lines on the canvas of your children's life.

The Father did not misinterpret when your prayers were not answered according to your specification. He understood precisely every explicit detail of your request. "Behold, the Lord's hand is not shortened, that it cannot save; neither his ear heavy, that it cannot hear." Isaiah 59:1 Not only does He hear every cry of his children; He also hears their every heartbeat. "He hears the prayer of the righteous." Proverbs 15:29 At the same time He hears your cry, He also sees the charted course ahead of you and your family.

Inability to comply on your terms is not the issue either. All power and authority sets upon His shoulders. Even the winds and seas obey at His command. As stated in Isaiah His hand is not too short to reach. He is fully equipped and qualified to answer according to your choosing. But, He has a far better plan ordained for you. "Trust in the Lord with all thine heart, and lean not unto thine own understanding. In all thy ways acknowledge him, and he shall direct thy paths." Proverbs 3:5-6

Never mistake a prayer answered differently than you had anticipated as an unanswered prayer. Nowhere in the Bible is there a mention of an unanswered prayer. The answer may be a resounding **Yes**, for which you are ecstatically grateful. A disappointing **No** at times will be the answer. But as faith arises, contentment replaces the disappointment. Many times the answer **Wait**, will be met with anticipation. Your patience may be stretched a bit as you wait. But in the end your faith may also be made a little stronger.

A lack of understanding may cloud your reasoning between good and bad. But God's wisdom is immeasurable. In His infinite wisdom He knows how to bless His children with good things. "Or what man is there of you, whom if his son ask bread, will he give him a stone? Or if he ask a fish, will he give him a serpent? If ye then, being evil, know how to give good gifts unto your children, how much more shall your Father which is in heaven give good things to them that ask him?" Matthew 7:9-11 In a sinful and evil nature, human beings still know how to lavish good gifts upon their children. Then all the more, a holy Father, who knows no sin, will bestow good things to those that ask of Him. "No good thing will he withhold from them that walk uprightly." Psalm 84:11 Human perception of good gifts versus bad makes all the difference in the world, like knowing the difference in a dot or a thorn.

Although it is His pleasure to give good things to His children, and to grant them the desires of their heart, His infallible love supercedes fulfilling your wish list. He takes greater pleasure in meeting your needs according to His divine wisdom, rather than your wants. Many snares and dangers may be lurking underneath your heart's desires, well hidden from you with your tunnel vision. However, nothing is hidden from His panoramic view. Granting your every wish according to your own demands, rather than His will, would sometimes place a big tarnish upon the painting canvas. Oh, and then would come the dreaded sanding process.

Jesus perfectly illustrated praying for God's will by the example, which He laid out in the Lord's prayer. "Thy will be done in earth, as it is in heaven." Matthew 6:10 And at the same time, He admonished His children to pray very specifically for their needs. "Give us this day our daily bread." Matthew 6:11 This displayed an example of asking God to grant a special need. Petitioning God to grant your own heart's desire is in order. "Be careful for nothing; but in every thing by prayer and supplication with thanksgiving let your requests be made known unto God." Philippians 4:6 Ask for specific needs to be met according to the will of the Father, precisely connecting you to your next appointed dot.

Prayerfully bringing your request unto the Father is to acknowledge your dependence upon him, not to bring your needs to His attention. He is already fully aware. "For your Father knoweth what things ye have need of, before ye ask him." Matthew 6:8 Neither should prayer be used to try to change God's mind, rather to conform and be submissive to His perfect will. Prayer should never be a means of aligning God's will with yours, but on the contrary, to align your will to His.

Ugly thorns can be turned into beautiful dots. "And we know that all things work together for the good of them that love God, to them who are the called according to his purpose." Romans 8:28 This scripture does not imply that everything that happens is life will be good. Rather that God will bring good out of bad situations. From inside the ugly bush of thorns planted along your way, God will paint a beautiful rosebush. The sufferings of life, He will bring to a good ending. This is a promise to all who love God and allow Him to place the dots and paint the picture of their life.

From the very matter that you are trying to fix, God may be painting a gorgeous rose, turning your ugly into pretty.

Sometimes, circumstances that seem to be a thorn in the side may simply be a roadblock, preventing you from flying over a hanging cliff, which you do not see. But, as the Father sees the dangling cliff before you, He will maneuver you back to safety. He sees every thorn, every roadblock, and every cliff along your path, as well as all the dots that He so perfectly designed for your walk of life.

Never curse your calamity, like the Israelites did. On numerous occasions God performed miracles of provision, protection, and deliverance for His special people on their journey to a special land of promise. Each new problem that they faced was certain to bring another round of whining, bickering, and downright rebellion. These were people who had a covenant relationship with God Almighty and a promise to enter into the promise land. Yet they focused more on their hardships, which many times were self-inflicted, than the promise that they had in God.

The Israelites suffered greatly at the hand of Pharaoh. Not because that God lacked the ability to stop Pharaoh. But, God allowed Pharaoh's heart to be hard against the children of Israel, refusing to let them go out of Egypt. Allowing the Egyptians to see God's signs and wonders was the purpose, not to make life miserable for the Israelites. "And the Egyptians shall know that I am the Lord, when I stretch forth mine hand upon Egypt, and bring out the children of Israel from among them." Exodus 7:5 Plagues they suffered, hardships they endured, but deliverance came by the hand of Almighty God. The Glory of God came bursting through each hard trial. The Israelites saw the dilemma facing them, while God saw His deliverance to the Israelites, and His glory being revealed to the Egyptians, with the Promised Land being the final picture. Dots lined their trail all the way to the wonderful promise that God had made to them. But, grumbling and murmuring all the way, they rebelled because the dots did not line up according to their liking.

In their own quandary, wallowing in self-pity, the Israelites failed to see that their crisis was nothing more than a bridge connecting their woes to the power of God and His glory. Glowing upon the canvas of a perfect painting will always be an image of the glory of God. The sight of His glory will be a beckoning call to others to come into His kingdom. Bringing others to know Him and the power of His might will always be the will of the Father.

Embrace each trial that comes your way as an opportunity for God to reveal His Glory, showing forth His power and might by signs and wonders. The final picture for the Israelites was not found in the plagues that came their way. The battles facing you and your family are not the final picture either. Look for the miraculous in every situation. God may miraculously change the circumstance or He may graciously endue you with strength to overcome. More importantly, His glory may be revealed to others who do not know Him. Through your toughest times, God may be doing a deeper work than meets your eye. He may be revealing His glory to other family members, friends, or even complete strangers, which you are unaware of. In your most horrendous crisis, the transparency of your faith may cause faith to arise within someone else. In your darkest moment, may His glory shine forth ever so brightly!

When embarking upon a dot of uncertainly, refuse to be tormented by fear. Not only will fear torture you, but will also paralyze you, leaving you in total despair. Cling more closely to your heavenly Father. Take a small child out of its comfort zone and watch as that child wraps around Mama or Daddy clinging ever so tightly, comforted by the loving arms holding them. Every child of God has a loving Father to hold them as well. Because of Him and His greatness, the righteous has nothing to fear. "He shall not be afraid of evil tidings: his heart is fixed, trusting in the Lord. His heart is established, he shall not be afraid, until he see his desire upon his enemies." Psalm 112:7-8 Unpleasant news may be received with sadness even grief, but, should never be met with fear, rather embraced with trust in Almighty God. The heart that is fixed and established in a steadfast faith in the Lord will know that God is bigger than the problem. But, the fearful heart will lose sight of the power and authority that God has over the crisis. Hang on; this is only a little dot of time. Soon the line will be drawn, connecting you to the next moment of time.

An extraordinary painting of dazzling beauty unfolds as all the dots are properly connected, as designed. Glittering through the backdrop will be a runner sprinting across the finish line into victory lane. Shinning through the canvas will be a mighty warrior, wearing a crown of victory. When the final lines have been drawn connecting each dot, the paintbrush has been laid aside, and the last drop of paint has dried, then will appear an indescribable picture, more marvelous than the human mind could even imagine. For now every race has been run, every battle has been fought, and victory has been won. What a beautiful sight to behold!

Who understands creation better than the creator? Who understands life better than the life giver? Who understands the language of love better than He who loved enough to die upon a cross for the world? Who understands the painting better than the painter? No one understands you better than He who holds you in the palm of His hand. He, who spoke creation into being by His voice, is the one who breathed life into your being, and His love reaches into the very depth of your soul. He is the one who has sketched out the portrait of your life. With paintbrush in hand, He is filling in all the creases and crevices with an assortment of colors. At times, you will wrench at the sanding. While at other times, you may rejoice as He smoothly brushes the paint over the canvas. Remember, the Father is the painter and He knows best how to bring to completion a perfectly, polished, finished portrait of life for all of His children. Along the way moving from dot to dot, He will smooth out the edges, heal broken hearts, and fix what you can't.

Chapter Six

In His Time

Society today is seeking instant gratification. Scores of people will do whatever it takes to satisfy their hungering desire for the wants of today and deal with the consequences tomorrow. While time may wait for no one, seemly no one wants to wait for time either. Bustling everywhere, hurry here and hurry there, things to do and places to go, people are constantly running in a mad rush, with no time to stop and smell the roses along the way. The busyness of life simple does not allow for any down time. No matter what the situation may be, the cry today is no waiting line please!

God's response is not so fast please. Just as every little dot has its own unique purpose; it also has an appointed time. "To every thing there is a season, and a time to every purpose under the heaven." Ecclesiastes 3:1 Along with purpose and plans, God also holds time in His hand. All things have a time to begin and a time for them to end. Keeping perfect time, His clock never runs too slow, nor does it run too fast. He will act according to His schedule and not yours. Just as important as trusting His will, you must also trust His timing.

Held in the hand of Almighty God are the times and seasons of the entire universe. Some mornings you awake to a bright sunshiny day without a cloud in the sky. Before the day's end you are running for cover as the sky darkens and raindrops begin to fall. Lightning bolts strike and the thunder rolls, ushering in a heavy downpour falling from the clouds. The howling wind may rage and hail may fall, as a severe storm blows in. But in due time the lightning stops, the sound of thunder no longer is in the air, no more hail falls from the sky and the rain dissipates. A colorful rainbow in its magnificent beauty replaces the dark clouds that once filled the sky. The majestic happenings of the day have been well orchestrated and timed in perfect unison with God's plan.

On a more personal level, times and seasons of your life are held in His hand as well. "My times are in thy hand." Psalm 31:15 Storms will come and go in your life turning good times into bad. Laughter may suddenly be silenced and flowing from your eyes will be a bucket of tears. Afraid to peep out, you wish you could keep your head under the covers. But in the appropriate time the clouds will evaporate, the brightness of the sunshine will appear and a beautiful rainbow will spread across your sky. Instead of promising that you would always have a rainbow, God promised to be with you through every dark cloud. Keep your eyes focused upon Him instead of your gloomy circumstance. Then just at the right time a beautiful rainbow will emerge from that dark and dreary cloud.

Just as every purpose has a specific time; God's timing also has a specific purpose. Rest assured, His plans and timing are for your good and His glory. Growth, development and maturity come through a process of time. The little fuzzy caterpillar may not be nearly as appealing to the eye as the colorful butterfly. But the magnificent splendor of the butterfly comes as a result of the development and growth of the caterpillar. The purpose of the caterpillar stage is so that the butterfly can reach its full potential. Through a period of time, real beauty comes sparkling by on the wings of a butterfly.

Granted growing pains are no fun, but they are necessary. Daydreams of adulthood may swirl over and over through the imagination of a child. But it is impossible to reach adulthood without the young and tender growing years. Skipping over the process of growing up would be a major disadvantage to anyone. Losing out on the lessons of life that are learned during the formative years would be shameful. Oftentimes waiting upon the Lord to move may be your growing time, as well. Missing out on the growth and maturity developed through a progression of time would also be a grave disservice to you.

Although you know your children are growing older, sometimes you wonder if they will ever grow up. Their maturity level seems to be spiraling downward. Though once sweet and innocent, they have now become a monster living in your house. Their behavior may be downright ugly. By the way, at this point in their life, they know much more than you ever knew. But as time goes by, lessons of life that they learn will help them to grow and develop into a mature individual. In time, your ugly duckling becomes a beautiful swan. Then suddenly, you will find yourself surmising how quickly time has passed.

Blossoming into a beautiful bloom is a product of time, along with some pampering and grooming. Gazing out your window, adoring your gorgeous flower garden so well displayed midst your beautiful landscaping, may simply be breathtaking. Hours have been spent cultivating the ground, watering, maybe even fertilizing. Carefully pulling up weeds while making sure the flowers stayed firmly in place, you have groomed your beautiful garden of flowers. Resting before your eyes now is a beautiful sight, which took time, work, grooming and pampering. The beauty of your exquisite garden will remain a work in progress. While it may lie dormant in the wintertime, once spring is in the air, grooming time has arrived again.

Esther, along with all the other young maidens who were eager to become queen, went through a process of grooming for one full year, before they were ever presented to the king. With perfumes, cosmetics, and oil of myrrh each young lady had been pampered. Well groomed and refined, Esther won the favor of the king. After a tedious process of grooming, she was crowed queen. While the palace was grooming Esther to be queen, God was grooming her for a much more important task. Using her position as royal queen, God ordained Esther and set her up in the kingdom of the land at such a time. "and who knoweth whether thou art come to the kingdom for such a time as this?" Esther 4:14 The life of every Jew in the nation was spared because of the influence that Esther had with the king. Esther's reign as queen was for a divine purpose and a designated time. Nonetheless, preparation had to be made through a time of grooming.

When it seems that you cannot move forward. Seemly all of life has either come to a halt or moving backwards. As you wait, time seems to be longer and longer. This may just be the time that you are in God's grooming parlor. During this waiting time, as you are being groomed, learn to listen to His still small voice and follow Him. Stepping in line with a herd of well-groomed sheep, following the shepherd, is better than flying with a flock of wild geese.

Mama, your children are certain to have their time in God's grooming parlor, as well. Standing on the sidelines, you may have an urge to rush in and fix them up in a hurry. Mama, you do not need to drag your youngsters out of the grooming parlor before the grooming is done.

Seasons of testing your faith, which tries your patience, are sure to arise from time to time. As your faith comes up against the blazing flames of fire, you quiver and tremble and sweat pours from your brow. Once the smoke had drifted away, and the ashes are blown to the side, a beautiful jewel surfaces as a result of the purifying process. Stunning in all of its beauty a gorgeous piece of ceramic would be worthless if time spent in the fiery furnace was omitted. The firing process adds strength and durability to a weak and fragile piece of artwork. Likewise trying times may strengthen your faith and build your character. "Wherein ye greatly rejoice, though now for a season, if need be, ye are in heaviness through manifold temptations: That the trial of your faith, being much more precious than of gold that perisheth, though it be tried with fire, might be found unto praise and honor and glory at the appearing of Jesus Christ." 1 Peter 1:6-7 But, in His time, the flames burn out, and the radiance of your beauty shines a little brighter. Times of refining and polishing your character while raising your faith to a new level oftentimes will overstep the boundaries of your comfort zone, and will most likely exceed your self allotted time frame.

Mom, you may patiently endure your own suffering. But the sufferings of your children are quite another matter. Restlessness invades your thoughts, pushing your nerves to the edge. Your heart aches and throbs as though it is being dragged through a thicket of thorns. With no time to wait, a quick fix is in high demand. If only you could, with a snap of the finger or the blink of an eye, you would fix it in a flash.

Though painful it may be to sit a spell upon an old thorn bush, or to sweat through the sweltering heat of the fire, jumping ahead of God can be even more painful. Leaping too quickly may just cause a crash landing. Rushing God can mess up the rosebush that He is trying to paint from inside the thorn bush.

Trying to force a fix before God's timing created a real catastrophe for Abraham and Sarah. Discontented to wait any longer, Sarah gave up on God's timing. She convinced Abraham to lie with her maiden, Hagar. Discouraged, Sarah decided that a son was not going to be born any other way. What a mess this created! Hagar conceived and birthed a son, named Ishmael. Years later the promised son, Isaac was born unto Abraham and Sarah. Suddenly, a rage of jealous stirred within Sarah. Hate for the maiden and her son rose up, as Sarah looked upon the lad. Sarah's makeshift fix led to a family feud that until this day has not ended, and never will end as long as time is on this earth. Sarah rushing and getting ahead of God's timing changed the course of world events throughout all of time.

Certainly a miraculous act of God can happen with the blink of an eye, or He may choose to work through a process of time. A man approached Jesus who had a son that was at the point of death. In the fourth chapter of John the story unfolds as Jesus replied to the father to go on his way, his son would live. The son immediately was made whole. The very next chapter of John paints a picture of a man who had suffered an infirmity for thirty-eight years before Jesus healed him. God was not limited by any time restraints. God deserves all the glory, honor and praise no matter if He takes thirty-eight years, thirty-eight minutes, or thirty-eight seconds. Remember, God works on His clock, not yours.

Playing over and over in this Mom's head were visions of her little infant crawling across the floor as he reached a few months old. Maybe by his first birthday, he would hold her hand as he learned to balance himself and take his first few steps. Then soon he would be running and playing with his two older brothers. Imaginations of the perfect family could not get any better. A wonderful loving and caring husband and three healthy bouncing boys filled Mom's world.

About two months after the newest addition came into the world; discovery was made of a disease causing a bone deficiency, which thankfully only affected his tibia or calf bone. Henceforth the bone running through the calf of his leg was very fragile. At such a young age, he suffered a broken bone in his leg, which was the fault of nothing or nobody except the diseased bone that he had at birth. Of course, the leg had to be set and in a cast for quite some time. Unfortunately, this is not the end of the story. In an effort to treat the bone decay, which was the primary source of the problem, this little baby endured three surgeries by the time he was two years old.

Mom suffered through many trying days, submerging all of her energy and efforts in carrying for the needs of this child, along with caring for her other two children. Doctor appointments too numerous to count, one cast after another, two rods had to be put into his leg, and several different braces made up the first couple of years of this tiny little ones life. Not to be outdone, at age one, this little tot shuffled all around while wearing a brace with unbelievable mobility. Lugging a brace around, by the time that he reached eighteen months, he was walking. Challenging as this nightmare has been for this family, they have come through in great stride, excelling into victory lane by relying upon their faith in God, which has been made stronger through this trying time.

Much prayer has reached the throne of God on behalf of this little one. With great assurance, I can boldly and confidently know that God could have instantly touched this little baby and made him well all at once, avoiding all the pain and agony, experienced by both the baby and his entire family. On the other hand,

God chose to answer these prayers in His way and in His timing.

His Mother spoke real truth when she stated that this has shown them to focus on the positive and never on the negative. They realized the incredible love and support of their family and friends. Family members spent weeks at a time pitching in and helping. Daily dependence upon the Lord only strengthened their faith. As they leaned upon the Lord He sustained them through it all.

As they have walked through the stages of this ordeal, God has been along beside them every step of the way. As anxieties arose, He shielded them with calmness. As tiredness set in, He girded them with new strength. While the future may hold even more surgeries for this little guy, more challenging days lie ahead for this family. But, they will boldly face each new day with confidence because they know the source of their help. " I will lift up mine eyes unto the hills, from whence cometh my help. My help cometh from the Lord, which made heaven and earth." Psalm 121:1-2

By the way, at three years old now, he runs and plays like Mom dreamed that he would. Soon he will be kicking a soccer ball. Marching out on that soccer field, he is already a winner, whether he scores a goalie or not. Free to Run, he is no longer bound by a brace. God's diagnosis turned out better than the original prognosis. God working through medical care and a period of time made all the difference in the world.

Patiently wait upon the Lord to move. "Be still and know that I am God." Psalm 46:10 Remaining calm and quiet, while waiting on God, is not always easy, but it is very worthwhile. Sometimes hastily trying to get to the other side of problems results in action taken that further enhances the problem. Digging the hole deeper is another way of putting it. Why? Human nature says don't just stand still, do something. Waiting upon the Lord does not mean to sit idle, rather to seek Him with your whole heart and to rely upon Him with unwavering confidence. Complete trust waits upon the Lord with a restful spirit and the mind at ease, instead of anxiously fretting in distress. Instead of exhausting all of your energy trying to fix what is beyond your control, channel this energy in praying, seeking, and trusting in the Lord.

God will strengthen, refresh and renew your soul as you wait upon Him. "But they that wait upon the Lord shall renew their strength; they shall mount up with wings as eagles; they shall run, and not be weary; and they shall walk, and not faint." Isaiah 40:31 Mounted up in the strength of the wings of an eagle, you can soar above anything that comes against you. On the other hand, running ahead of God just may clip that wing bringing you to a fall. Standing out from all the other birds, the eagle has a more evenly broad wingspan for a more direct and faster flight, making for fewer obstacles, and a speedier journey through the rough terrain.

Put your running shoes on! He has strengthened you to move forward as you wait upon Him. You will run and not grow weary. You shall continue to walk until you have walked right over this mountain. You will not faint by the wayside. So, wait upon the Lord. Pray and wait for his guidance before you take action contrary to his plan.

What seems to be God's delay may be a dusty trail leading to your divine destiny. Seemly the clock had struck midnight, time had run out, Jesus had arrived too late, so Mary and Martha thought. After all, four days had passed since their brother Lazarus had died. What could Jesus do now? But the divine appointment for Lazarus was to be raised from the dead, while Mary, Martha and the other Jews divinely witnessed the resurrection. God was right on time for the miracle that He had on His mind.

Your clock is about to strike midnight and time is running out, so it seems. You have prayed and waited upon God. Each new day finds you looking for a ray of hope. Crying out to God every night, as you bow your head and your knees hit the floor, searching for an answer. Just remember, time never runs out on God. His clock will not strike midnight until He comes to carry His children home.

Sometimes hindrances come slithering upon your path from an evil force. Daniel prayed and fasted for twenty-one days as he awaited his answer. Revealed unto Daniel on the twenty-fourth day was the assurance that an angel was sent forth on his behalf the very first day that he had prayed. But an evil being had stood in opposition against the angelic being that was bringing forth his answer. Reinforcement came;

overpowering the enemy and Daniel's prayer was answered.

Just like Daniel, hindering spirits may stand between you and your answer at times. But, just like help came to Daniel, as you stand firm in your faith, your adversary, Satan will be defeated, and your answers will come too. Spoken in authority by the name of Jesus Christ, you have the privilege and the power to command that he back off and he has to run. Though your voice may seem small, Satan hears the sound of the entire kingdom of God running rampant over him, causing demonic spirits to fall powerless, as you speak the name of Jesus.

The three weeks of waiting time for Daniel was not wasted time. He spent this time in prayer and fasting, seeking the Lord. Intensely waiting upon the Lord with such sincerity of heart serves to strengthen faith, build character and create a more intimate relationship with the heavenly Father. Daniel was never out of God's sight. And in the right moment of time, victory came forth.

Your family will always be a work in progress. Tides will roll in and out throughout the course of life. How long you may ask before the tide changes? Since every purpose has a time, and time has a purpose, your tide probably will not change until the purpose has been fulfilled. Then rolling out from underneath the tide will be a piece of artwork of sheer beauty. "He hath made every thing beautiful in his time." Ecclesiastes 3:11 Wait upon the Lord. He will move in His time.

Chapter Seven

The Missing Piece

Little pieces, big pieces, various shapes, colors and designs, puzzles come together when all the right pieces are linked together. Many stories may be told and beautiful scenery displayed by connecting all of the pieces one by one. Puzzles may come in ten pieces or thousands. No matter the number of pieces, the picture cannot be completed if one piece is missing. Oh the frustration of working ever so long and hard, studying and matching all the right pieces of a thousand piece puzzle to find that you only have nine hundred and ninety-nine pieces. You have just put together a puzzle with a hole that cannot be filled in. You may disassemble and rearrange, try over and over again, but in the end this is still a puzzle with one missing piece.

Like a puzzle, life flows much better when all the pieces fall in place. Like many other Mothers in today's society, you too may be facing the challenge of working a puzzle with a missing piece. That wonderful knight and shining armor that you married may have walked out on you, leaving you in total despair, wondering how you will ever juggle the affairs of your family.

Although, you may have tried very hard and was committed to your marriage, the man of your dreams simply was not committed to you. Shattering all of your dreams, he chose another trail of life, which did not include you. If children are involved, they may be looking to Mama for an explanation. But, Mama has no answers. Through your own puddle of tears, you try to assure your children that all will be well. How badly you wish that you could fix the aching little hearts and dry the tears of the little ones left clinging to your apron strings. Feeling rejected, torn and tattered, you try to piece together all the brokenness left behind. Your heart yearns to put the puzzle together. But no matter how hard you try, one piece is still missing.

Analyzing every little detail since the day you met your handsome Mr. Charming, and all the reasoning in the world may never help you to understand why you were kicked to the curb. But, one thing is for certain that you need to know, YOU ARE NOT FORSAKEN! God has said, "I will never leave thee, nor forsake thee." Hebrews 13:5 Though, your deserting husband may have abandoned you, God never will. He will make smooth the rocky road that you must travel. He will caress you in your time of stress. "In my distress I cried unto the Lord, and he heard me." Psalm 120:1." His ear will be open to your every cry and His arms will tenderly hold you in the midnight hours.

As your spouse became a missing piece of the home, most likely so did his income. Although he may pay child support, you may still come up short in the finance department. Worries over bills and basic needs of the family will certainly compound the stress that you are already under. Denying yourself a few of the luxuries that you have been accustomed to is not so bad. But, oh the pain of explaining to your children that they cannot have that new bicycle or computer game that they have so desperately wanted. You may be struggling to simply put a meal on the table and clothes on their back, which by the way, may not be brand name anymore.

Sharing time with the children may be another issue that goes against your liking. Now they shuffle from your home to Dad's new home, possible even a new wife. Now that the kids are off to visit Dad, you may welcome a little bit of serene time. But, as time goes by your house becomes all too quiet. In all the stillness, your mind races from one scene to the next concerning the welfare of your little ones. If they get hurt, Mama wants to be the only one who applies the band-aid. Should they get sick, you want to check the fever and administer the baby aspirin, instead of someone else. What gets broken, Mama wants to fix. Bath time leaves you wondering if they got their hair shampooed, the little ears cleaned, and all the dirt in between their toes washed away. Did they say their nighttime prayers before going off to sleep?

Many times when children are shared between two different homes, family life is quite different from one home to the next. This may result in the children having two sets of guidelines to live by. The forbidden rules of your house do not apply while visiting Dad, possibly creating confusion and a lack of self-control within the children. Two worlds collide when parents teach their children two different paths of life. Opposing principles leading your children may very well lead them onto a destructive path. When the other parent refuses to cooperate in teaching and discipline, you must still put out your best effort, and pray, pray, pray!

Not all divorces end with a lifetime of fighting, and pulling the family in different directions. Being separated by a divorce, my sister and the father of her son chose to cooperate with one another, consulting with each other; they made decisions together concerning their child. Discipline was agreed upon. In other words, he could not be in trouble with one parent and easily slide off the hook with the other parent. They both participated in the upbringing of their son. Christmas morning has always found them celebrating together. The father has graciously been invited to come to my sister's house every Christmas all through the years, an invitation that he has also graciously accepted. By the way, she has a twenty-year marriage with another fine gentleman, who has been just as gracious in this matter. Attaining to such cooperation requires a combined effort from all parties involved.

Rearing children is not an easy task for anyone. But, for the single Mom, the challenge may become even more daunting. With a companion missing out of your life, you may have a few more hurdles to jump. Surmounting on top of you may be a few more problems that seem to be beyond your limited resources, capabilities, or strength. Basically, you started a partnership business, but the partner flew the coop, leaving you with all the duties. Or quite possibly, he was such a scoundrel that you could not live with him and you kicked him out. Either way, your puzzle has a missing piece. Take courage, God knows your circumstance, and has no limitation, and He is never missing in action.

Working around the missing piece, the puzzle of your life now takes on a new shape. Once that you have gathered together all of the scattered pieces, you begin linking all of the same colors and shapes again, creating a brand new way of life. On the other side of every ending, a new beginning is waiting to unfold.

On the other hand, your marriage may have been made in heaven. An endless cord of love bound your two hearts together so strong that it could not be broken. As he held you in his arms and you looked into his eyes, you knew that he cherished you as much as you treasured him. While a divorce would never separate the two of you, he may have been snatched away in an instant by some horrible tragedy. Or some lingering illness may a slowly taken him away.

Life has just left you with a deep dark hole. No matter how much fullness that your children, friends, or other family member add to your life, you are still engulfed with an emptiness that seemingly cannot be filled. Drudgery looms over your head as you face each new day. Rising up in the morning you may take a shower, get dressed, brush your teeth, comb you hair, and fix you face with plenty of make-up, but you still feel incomplete. Never in your wildest imagination, did you ever dream that you would be left with this missing piece of your life, leaving such a void spot in your heart. Truly part of you is now missing.

In the very depth of your soul, a pain that seems to have been permanently seared with a hot iron is your daily companion. As the sun fades, a sense of loneliness nestles in to nest with you throughout the entire night. Nighttime seems to bring more doom than the morning did. No mate to lay your head down with and no one to share in your dreams. All the plans that the two of you shared have now crumpled into a pile of rubbish. Gone are the big strong arms that used to hold you. As the days turn into weeks, and the weeks into months, this vicious cycle of aching and loneliness does not leave your side.

Ringing in your ears a thousand times are the questions of why and how did this happen. Agonizing over ever little what if this or what if that, you wonder what should have been to what could have been, only bringing you back to the question of why. When no reply comes from all of your questioning, then you are haunted by the silence. In all of your questioning, never question the sovereignty of God. Some questions will never be answered in this life and once you enter through the gates of heaven, the concerns and worries of this life will not be important anymore.

The really big question lingering over your head is What Next, as you wonder what is around the next bend. Although your future may be uncertain, you can be certain of the God of your future. When the ground underneath your feet is shaking, He will be the firm foundation on which your feet can stand. "I waited patiently for the Lord; and he inclined unto me, and heard my cry. He brought me up also out of a horrible pit, out of the miry clay, and set my feet upon a rock, and established my goings." Psalm 40:1-2 He will set you upon a path and make your way steadfast. Just as a horse cannot be made to drink from the water trough which it is led to, God will not force you to walk on the path that he leads you to either. The choice is yours to make, whether to wonder in the wilderness or to allow God to direct your steps.

Though you may be frightened out of your wits at times, do not allow yourself to become entangled in a web of fear! "For God hath not given us the spirit of fear; but of power, and of love, and of a sound mind." 2 Timothy 1:7 Instead of fear, God has given you the power to conqueror fear. Do not allow the sound mind that God gave to you to become cloudy with fear, causing irrational thinking. Numerous times God has spoken through scripture "Fear Not." The only antidote to fear is trusting in God.

Settling in the hearts of your little ones is a missing piece as well. Daddy will not be there to hold them by the hand, to teach them to play ball, or to help you tuck them in bed at night. Grief-stricken, you try to comfort and bring a sense of normalcy to your family. In your desperation, as you struggle to console your children, remember that each child is a unique individual, with their own personality and special traits. They will grieve in their own unique manner. Therefore, what may be most soothing to one child may be quite disturbing to one of their siblings. Helping each child to find the best coping mechanism tailored to meet their need is of utmost importance. Please do not underestimate the benefit of counseling or support groups. People who have been trained to help others in time of sorrow can be a blessing to you and your family. They may quickly discover each one's personality and match them up with their best grieving method. Mama cannot pick up all the pieces and put everything back in place. A missing piece has left your family broken and wracked with pain, and Mama cannot fix it.

Missing from the table is one plate where Dad used to dine. Dread hangs over your family as mealtime approaches. That empty chair is a grim reminder of the loss that your family has suffered. In the quietness, you try to eat, and then choking back tears, the appetite simply disappears. Then one day, the silence is broken, and conversation around the table is a welcome sight. Reminiscing of times when Dad joined the circle at dinnertime will begin to warm the hearts of those left behind. Precious memories can be healing to the broken heart.

Yes, this puzzle of your life is broken and cannot be mended, but you are not defeated. God will give you a brand new puzzle! He will shape, mold and polish all the little torn pieces, and then begin linking them together one piece at a time. Sadly, this new puzzle forms around a big gapping hole right in the middle of your heart. As time goes by, memories begin to fill in the gap. Strangely, thoughts of yesterday may erase some of the pain of today. The remembrance of a funny incident of the past may bring a smile to your face, or even a big walloping round of laughter. Many times, I have listened to someone share a hilarious story involving a deceased loved one that brought tears of laughter to their face. With this laughter also came healing to their soul, and in the process another layer suddenly filled in that empty spot in the heart.

Eventually, another fine gentleman may come along and take up a place in your heart. But, he will never replace the missing one. Remember giving birth to your first child. How your heart was so filled with love for this little one. You beamed with pride as you held that new little baby. But, then the second child came, possible even third or fourth and you experienced the same amount of love, joy, and pride each time. One child never replaced the love that you had for the others. Your heart only grew bigger, making room for another. The same is true now in your new circumstance, your new puzzle. Although you may love again, your first love will never be replaced. Your heart will only broaden, making room for another.

As you begin to go down the road of life with this other person, refuse to take a trip down the road called guilt. Having lost a wonderful, loving husband, one grieving wife carried a huge load of guilt once she began to date again. Thinking that she was not being true to the commitment that she had made to her deceased husband, put a damper on her newfound love. Her wedding vows had stated, "until death do us part." The day that they became separated by death, her commitment had been completed. As long as there was breath in his body, she had been faithful, well serving her commitment. She was plagued by feelings that even a little joy and happiness in her life now was surely a great injustice to that one that had loved her so deeply and was no longer here. Enjoying life without him just seemed so wrong, maybe down right disrespectful to the mate that she had so adored. Embracing the new puzzle that life now offers you, shows no disgrace and is no reflection of the love that you shared with the first love of your life. While these feelings are natural instincts, they are also thoughts that need to be kicked to the curb. Life must go on, happiness must be found again, or you will become so entangled in a web of grief that cannot be shaken, and will choke the life out or you. While, I am not suggesting that another marriage is a must, you certainly have the freedom to make that choice.

Though your children may adapt, a missing link will always be apart of their life. As they go through life, on occasions they will wonder what would Dad do if he were here, or what would he say concerning a specific issue. Your strong-armed athletic son may become the star quarterback of his high school football team. Missing from the stands will be his number one fan. As he stands with arm raised, ready to throw the ball, a thought of Dad may cross his mind. That pass is thrown with much more vigor, going farther down the field. Knowing how proud Dad would be adds to the thrill of the moment for that son.

Your beautiful little girl may become the homecoming queen. As she stands on the field glowing in all of her beauty, oh how she quietly wishes that Daddy could be there to see. But, that can not be, because Dad is the missing piece of this special event. As Dad rushes through her mind, a lump may arise in her throat. Then her eyes may sparkle a little brighter and her smile becomes a little wider, knowing how proud he would be to see her now. Along comes prom and graduation day, another special moment without Dad. Amidst all the excitement, a little sadness will mingle in, because someone is missing.

Amidst all the grief, turmoil, confusion and emptiness, may you, as well as your children, find consolation in knowing that God is your strength, your shelter, your sustainer. " A father of the fatherless, and a judge of the widows, is God in his holy habitation." Psalm 68:5 God is taking special notice of your family because you have special needs. He desires to heal the brokenness of your family. "He healeth the broken in heart, and bindeth up their wounds." Psalm 147:3

Whether through divorce or death, you have become a single Mom with that special someone missing out of you life, and your heart is very heavy. Matching your heavy heart, your load of responsibilities has become heavier. You are shouldering the weight of the family with no mate to hold up his end of the load. A team of two horses may pull a wagon quite easily. But, release one horse from the team and the load becomes much heavier for the one horse left standing. In spite of the weight hanging over you, remember that nurturing the children must take precedence all over other matters. You can replace a burned out light bulb, repair a broken appliance or mow the overgrown grass much easier than you can fix a broken spirit in a young child.

While it seems that you are a one-horse carriage plowing through life all alone, remember that Jesus sticks with you through thick or thin. "There is a friend that sticketh closer than a brother." Proverbs 18:24 This friend called Jesus invites you to bring your heavy load and the burden of your heart to him. "Come unto me, all ye that labor and are heavy laden, and I will give you rest. Take my yoke upon you, and

97

learn of me; for I am meek and lowly in heart: and ye shall find rest unto your souls. For my yoke is easy, and my burden is light." Matthew 11:28-30 This is a beckoning call to ALL who are weighed down with a heavy burden, to come and allow him to give rest to the weary soul. Allowing Him to bear your burden is sure to lighten your load. In essence, He harnesses up to your carriage and become the horse pulling the load. Then you are free to trot along life's trail much more at ease.

Little pieces, big pieces, coming together one by one, are forming a new puzzle. One set of circumstances connected to another, creating one small piece at a time. In this new puzzle new faces are sure to appear. However, they will weave in and connect with familiar faces of the past. Different people who come and go across your path will simply add to the variety of pieces, piecing together this new puzzle. Whether you move to a new location or stay in the same place, home will surely be a huge piece of the puzzle. Included in this new puzzle are memories of the past, but plans for your future must be inserted as well. One thing is for certain, if you will allow God to join together all the pieces in His way and in His timing, life can be beautiful again, not only for you, but for your children, as well.

Chapter Eight

Letting Go

Perhaps your baby took the first few steps by holding to your hand, maybe the sofa or a table. Then the day came that as you stood that little bundle of joy up, you held on firmly, helping the little one to gain some balance, and then you let go. Encouragement came from you, as you coaxed the little feet to move, by repeating over and over "come to Mommy." Walking unassisted for the first time, those precious little feet brought a round of cheers from the whole family. You clapped and clapped, and yelled Hey, Hey, while a grin spread across your face a mile wide. Mama letting go of that precious little hand made this day possible. Before long, you were busy, chasing that little tot all over the house.

How badly letting go hurt, the first day that you had to send your young one off to school or to some daycare center. Tears welled up within your eyes as you said good-by on that dreaded day. After all, Mama Hen couldn't be their watching over her little chick. Letting go meant trusting someone else to care for your most prized treasure. Pain can be eased and sorrows lessen by entrusting your children into the care of God.

As time rolls on, you could not possible count the days that you wore the hat of taxicab driver. Trips galore as you drove them from one event to the next occasion. From one friend's house to another, you would drive, no matter how tired you were. From shopping malls to the candy store you went. All the while you were wondering if this ever end. Then the most awful thing happened. You found yourself driving to the nearest driver license office, knowing that the return trip back home would find you riding in the passenger seat.

That evening your heart skipped a few beats as you stood in the driveway and watched that car drive off without you. You must now get control of the wave of emotions running up and down your spine that was sparked by letting go of the keys. One moment pride has you gloating with your head held high. The next moment, you seem to be swallowed up by fear, and your head hung down in prayer. Should you hear a siren before that car returns, you wait for a phone call in a panic, prepared to rush to the hospital to your mangled up child.

Letting go brings tears of joy, moments of laughter along with tears of sadness and moments of horror. Of all the horror stories you could tell, and all the dreadful thoughts that letting go could muster up, none could be quite as horrendous as the story that baby Moses Mother could share. Imagine her horror, realizing that her baby boy had a death sentence upon him at birth. "And Pharaoh charged all his people, saying, every son that is born ye shall cast into the river, and every daughter ye shall save alive." Exodus 1:22 Tossed into the river to drown was to be the fate of all Hebrew male babies. What was she to do? How could she spare her baby's life?

Managing to hide her little baby Moses for three months, it became impossible to keep him hidden any longer. Imagine her heartache as she made a little basket, put her baby inside and released him into the river. His older sister stood by and watched to see what would become of her little baby brother. Letting go must have been so difficult on that day. But, his Mother knew that releasing him was the only way that his life could be spared. Holding on to her baby would have definitely resulted in his death. With her back against the wall, she could do nothing but let go and trust God. God had big plans for Moses, much bigger than anything that his Mother could have fathomed.

As Pharaoh's daughter came to bathe in the river, she spotted the baby, and was moved with much compassion, and wanted him as her own son. At the request of Pharaoh's daughter, Moses very own sister was asked to find a Hebrew woman to nurse the child and that she would pay wages to the nursing Mother. Of course, his own Mother enjoyed the pleasure of nursing him. After nursing and weaning her baby, letting go must have ripped Mama's heart out as she handed little Moses over to Pharaoh's daughter to rear up as her own son. While God made preparations to use Moses as the one who would lead the Israelites out of Egypt, Mama had to let go. But God held little Moses in the palm of His hand and He well preserved His divine plan that He had for him.

And then there was Hannah, who letting go of her little Samuel went to a greater depth than most Mothers ever experience. Hannah was in great sorrow and distress because she was childless. "The Lord has shut up her womb." 1 Samuel 1:5 She prayed until she had poured her whole heart and soul out before the Lord. God granted her request and blessed her with a son, whom she named Samuel. (The name Samuel means because I have asked of the Lord.) From the deepest yearnings of her heart, she cried and pleaded with the Lord to open her womb and allow her to bare children.

"For this child I prayed; and the Lord hath given me my petition which I asked of him: Therefore also I have lent him to the Lord; as long as he liveth he shall be lent to the Lord. And he worshiped the Lord there." 1 Samuel 1:27-28 Hannah made a little coat for Samuel each year and brought it to him when she came to make yearly sacrifices. Hannah had made a commitment that once Samuel had been weaned, she would bring her precious little son and offer him up unto God, leaving him with Eli, the priest, to do the work of the Lord. Thus, resolving that once a year she would visit her child, which she had so desperately longed for. "Samuel was established to be a prophet of the Lord." 1 Samuel 3:20 Without hesitation, Hannah made a tremendous sacrifice by letting go of her son and releasing him unto the Lord. Instead of watching her son grow from day to day, she was content to watch him grow from year to year, so that the will of God could be fulfilled. While Hannah let go, she knew that Samuel was in good hands.

God is not asking you to bring your child to the church office, drop it off, and come to visit once a year. Nonetheless, some things He is asking you to turn loose and let go. God wants you to let go of the worrisome burdens that rob you of your joy and peace, sucking the life out of you. Bring unto the Lord all those seemly unfixable problems that overwhelm you, and see what God can do. He can fix what you can't.

Some situations may call for the removal of your hands, before God can fix it according to His plan. Just as Hannah trusted completely in the Lord to give her a child, she was just as confident that He would take care of her son. By faith, you can release your children to the care of the Almighty one. Let go of your worries and fears by trusting in His providential care for your family. Then like Hannah you can know that your children are in good hands.

Let go of your selfish dreams and ambitions for your children. Refrain from trying to live out your own life's dream through the life of your children. They must be allowed to dream their own dream, dance their own dance, and live their own life. However, in order that they may live out their God given purpose, pray that their dreams will be in alignment with His divine plan. He created each individual with specific talents and abilities for a particular purpose. Therefore, imposing your own ambitions upon your children may hinder them from fulfilling God's plan for their life. Relinquish your will and ask for His will to be done! Hannah's only desire for Samuel was that he would be a useful servant in the kingdom of God.

Releasing your children unto the Lord does not exempt you from your responsibilities, resulting in neglecting them. God blessed you with your little ones. While at the same time, He bestowed upon you a huge responsibility to lovingly care for them. Parenting them, by the grace of God, still rests upon your shoulders. Your responsibilities to your children are not to be taken lightly. The duties of Mom may seem to be endless. As Mom, you serve as caregiver, leader, instructor, teacher of many subjects. You must nurture, nourish, cloth, and set guidelines, to name a few.

In the role of Motherhood, plenty of crucial matters are at stake. Important issues deserve your undivided attention. Don't' sweat the small stuff. Let go of the trivia matters that will only deprive you of valuable time and boggle your mind, hindering you from addressing the more weighty matters that are at hand.

Let go of the past. You cannot look forward with your face turned backward. Certainly, past experiences offer up valuable lessons. But drowning in a sea of guilt over past failures will assuredly be a stumbling block for the future. Crying over yesterday's disappointments will rob you of today's joy, while tomorrow's triumphs may be lost at sea. Hold on to the valuable lessons that the past has taught you. But, let go of yesterday's junk, and look to the future with a bright hope.

After years of lovingly caring for your children, teaching, guiding, disciplining, and meeting their every need, letting go is not easy. You have changed diapers, warmed bottles, bathed babies, cooked meals, washed dishes, and done mountain loads of laundry. As they grew you helped with homework, attended PTA meetings, and attended many other functions.

Then the day comes, when they are all grown up, and Mama has been released from the above duties. What a culture shock! Mom feels lost and empty. But, as every bird leaves the nest, most likely your children will also leave home, creating the empty nest syndrome for you as well. Letting go is not a time for moping, moaning and groaning. You must get on with life.

While you are released from certain duties that you have performed in the past, never consider yourself as resigned from your position as Mama. The role of Mama now takes on a different look. You may have fixed broken toys, mended favorite clothing items, bandaged cuts and scrapes, and helped them to restore relationships with some of their friends after a spout. You probably have dried some tears and patched their broken hearts a few times. Quite frankly, you with the guidance of the Holy Spirit have served as the chief fixer of all that was broken. You must now step back and allow them to be captain of their own affairs.

All the years of teaching and guidance should have prepared them to face life, deal with the issues that come, fix what they can, and leave the rest to God. They most definitely will face difficult circumstance along the way, some that they cannot fix, and neither can you. Nevertheless, if they have established a rock solid faith, then their trust in God will see them through. Either God will fix the problem, or His grace will carry them through the trial.

Good choices, bad choices, life is full of both. Even the wisest and most prudent people have fallen prey to a few bad ideas. But, choices we all must make. In the past, you have made choices for your children, which left them with no alternative. And at other times you gave them the freedom to make their own choice. A time for the changing of the guard has now arrived. The freedom and responsibility for making choices now belongs to the adult child. However, you may be granted the privilege of offering some guidance and insight into their decision-making. You certainly are blessed with the liberty to pray and intercede to the Lord, asking God to direct their thoughts and to lead their steps.

While, you may offer words of wisdom, be careful not to force your opinion. Good sound advice offered lovely and sparingly, may be appreciated. However, a strongly suggested opinion, repeated over and over will become annoying. Unlike when they were younger and you took charge, being in control is no longer an option for you. Like everyone else, they are sure to make mistakes from time to time. When you see a big pitfall in the making, you may point out the dangers that you see. But, the ultimate decision is not yours to make. You have been let go from your assignment as the authoritarian.

Trying to force your own will upon your children will most likely provoke your children to anger. Never attack your children's ability to make decisions. Consequently, this sort of an attack may devour their sense of value, leaving them feeling worthless, good for nothing, and unintelligent. Although, a polite conversation, addressed in a loving manner, voicing your concerns regarding their affairs may be in order. But, in the end, their decision must be respected.

Naturally, like most other parents, you want to see your children succeed in life. Mom, you may have envisioned your child highly educated, entering a career that earns big bucks. The career path, which they follow, must be their choice and not yours. Should they choose a career, not as admirable as you would like, please be supportive of their decision, unless their actions are illegal, unethical, or immoral. And worse yet, if they choose not to work, do not support them financially, thus allowing them to suffer the consequences of that bad choice.

While growing up their social life needed some direction from you. While, you may not necessarily have picked their friends for them, certain guidelines needed to be followed. Warning them to choose friends of good character was of utmost importance. Most assuredly, you should have steered them away from the gang members, vandalizing the town, harassing the neighbors, and any other undesirable activities. Choosing friends will now be completely their choice. But, you are not prohibited from praying that they will seek out friends of notable character. Pray that they not be misguided by any evil influences.

In the earlier years of dating, your permission may have been demanded on their choice of a date. Just any shabby creature knocking on your door to escort your daughter out would not have been acceptable. Your son bringing home the girl with the worst reputation in town did not carry your stamp of approval either. But, they now have reached an age that they will make their own choice concerning dating. Trust that the guidelines that you instilled within them earlier in life, will now guide their heart-thumping emotions.

Tread lightly when you disapprove of their choice of a dating partner. Bear in mind, that one day this person could possibly join your family. Harsh words of the past can tarnish your relationship with your child and their spouse. You do not live in a time or a place where parents arrange a spouse for their children. The choice is in their court, and that is the end of the story. Absolutely, positively, under no circumstance, are you privileged to choose a marriage partner for your child. However, accepting their choice of a mate with wide-open arms of love, welcoming the newest member into your family, is highly recommended. You may have prayed from the rock-a-by years through the toddling years and the teenage years that the road of life would lead your young into the waiting arms of their special mate. But, you cannot choose the mate.

While you may be the queen of your own castle, so are your sons and daughters the kings and queens of their habitat. Upon paying them a visit, you must remove your royal crown and let go of your reign. Being a guest does not deem you as temporary in charge. If you do not like the way the hand towel is hung, so what, it is not your towel to hang! You don't like the way the bed is made, it is not yours to sleep in. The kitchen is not laid out according to your liking, stay out of the kitchen. Entering into someone else's home, demanding that your own ways be carried out becomes demeaning and downright disrespectful.

Embarking upon the dreaded time for the young to begin life away from Mama's side, questions are sure to arise in Mama's heart. Have they reached the level of maturity necessary for this stage of life? How often will I see them now? Will they even miss me? Mom as you lay your head upon your pillow at night; often times you will wonder about the well being of each individual child. But, letting go and trusting them to the care of Almighty God will make this time less fretful for you.

From infant to adulthood, you have protected your children. Like any mother hen, your wings have shielded them from many dangers. Now, they will flee from the nest, no longer hidden under your protection. Truthfully, they were always under God's protection more than yours. When it comes time to let go, a real genuine faith in God will offer you confidence and peace of mind.

Mom, you may find it difficult to let go of your young for numerous reasons. Selfishness may hamper Mom's willingness to let go. After all, Mama has much invested, from labor pains to many sleepless nights. The long list continues on to the tears that you have shed, the hopes that you have built, then sometimes to see those hopes vanish like a melting piece of ice on a hot summer day. Your children are little lives that you have shaped, molded and formed like a potter from a heap of clay. Countless days, you have toiled for your family, with no end in sight. Seemingly a constant ritual of lying awake at night, mulling over this fix or that fix for your family, at times with no suitable fix to be discovered. Yes, Mama has much at stake. Mama wants to hold on because letting go is painful. Yet, the fruit of your labor is yet to be harvested. Watching your children strike out on their path of life, putting into practice those things that you have taught them is a time of joyful reaping.

Fear may keep Mama holding on with a tight grip. The mind can run rampant with thoughts of all sorts of horrible dangers just waiting to snag your beloved children. Who will guard and safely protect those, who are out from underneath Mama's wing? Trust in He who has a much greater wing span than you. "He shall cover thee with his feathers, and under his wings shalt thou trust: his truth shall be thy shield and buckler." Psalms 91:4 Trust in God's divine direction to lead your children around dangerous bends throughout the course of life. Let go of your fear and allow your faith in the Supernatural, Supreme Being of God Almighty to sustain you.

Another frightening thought is that they may walk away from the teaching that Mama has taught them. Evil influences may attack from all sides. Though they may walk away from Mama, they cannot get away from the unction and urging of the Holy Spirit. Pray against every evil force that tries to lure them off of the beaten path. Mama, they may try to side step your teachings, even try to shake it off completely. But, in the end you probably will find that those godly influences, which Mama buried deep within them, are not so easily destroyed. Again, let go of the fear, which will only serve to drag you down.

Take a deep breath, sigh and let go. Reminiscences of days gone by, when her three little girls were busy buzzing around the house so lovingly captured the heart of my own Mother until the day that she passed from earth to glory. Although, her three girls were all in their fifties at the time of her passing, she still often expressed how she missed having us at home. Taking us one by one upon her lap, snuggling us in her arms was some of her fondest memories throughout the years. Being surrounded by her family was as refreshing as a cool breeze on a spring like day. She never failed to tell both of my sisters and me how much she loved us and how proud we made her. But, in all of her love, when the time came to cut the apron string, she so graciously and unselfishly stepped aside. As she accepted each son-in-law with tender compassion, she knew that her children's place was to be with their husbands, which by the way, she also considered them as her sons. Although, my blissful wedding day meant a move of about eight hundred miles away, she wholehearted said good-by with her blessing. The process of letting go of three young girls gained her three sons and some grandchildren, and even great grandchildren. Oh, may I not fail to mention how she so doted over each grandchild.

As my own children now have grown into adulthood, I too have experienced the many different emotions associated with my young leaving the nest. Love still penetrates every fiber of my being for them. Like any Mother Peacock, a sense of pride fills my heart for my little flock as well. Their every accomplishment swells my heart a little bigger. Unreservedly, I am probably their number one cheerleader, cheering them on, as they pursue their hopes and dreams. Problems rising up to tackle them, grips this Mama's heart with pain also. Neither have I been spared from fear that all would be well with them. Positively, they know that Mama will be praying anytime they call with a problem. By the way, they have now blessed me with the grand joy of grandchildren. Most definitely Grandma is the biggest cheerleader and greatest fan of those little darlings. Thankfully, letting go does not mean loosing touch. Though our lives are lived out as separate individuals, yet still entwined, knitted together by love for each other.

Mama, you have filled many roles throughout the years. As nursemaid, you nursed them back to good health during times of sickness. With fevers racing upward you held them, cried and prayed. Accidents occurred, for a moment your heart stopped, and then you raced to their rescue, drying their tears, and consoling their fears. Then there were nights that your little ones awoke suddenly from a horrible nightmare. Mama went running to their bedside, held them, kissed them, and assured them. On occasions their little heart was broken, possibly by a crude remark from a friend, Mama was there to comfort. When frightened out of their wits, Mama always had a way of calming the fear away. Mama, you will not be there to dry every tear, nor soothe away the pain. You cannot catch every fall; neither can you fix every problem. But, you can confidently release them to the unfailing care of God. He will walk with them through places that you could never trod, down every valley, and over ever mountain, He shall carry them. Though they will leave your side, the heavenly Father will always be by their side.

Just because your children have reached adulthood does not mean that the final chapter has been closed on family trials. The heartaches of Mama do not end with the eighteenth birthday of the last child. Letting go is not the end, only a major milestone.

Letting go will probably spout a few more limbs to your family tree, as it continues branching out. Adding to the thrill of life, a new generation is born. This new generation comes glazed over with a few extra scoops of sugar and they are called grandchildren. Then you see the cycle of life begin all over again. Mama is now called Grandma. Lining your trail now is a new set of joys, and at the same time a new set of worries. Fretting over those little one just as much as you did your own, as you yearn to fix all that becomes broken in their little lives. Whether it is your children or you grandchildren, all that you cannot fix just let go and let God.

Chapter Nine

I Am that I Am

Carefully you would choose that special someone to watch over and care for your small children. Gathering all the information that you could, proving their trustworthiness before dropping off your children, to leave in their care. Confidently you may release your family to the one who is called I Am That I Am. His power has been tested and proven time and time again, and has never failed, revealing His infallible love by the way of the cross. Helping to carry your load, all through the child rearing years, then when time comes for your young to take wings and fly, letting go becomes much easier by releasing them into His tender loving arms.

A shoulder strapped with worries and woes becomes a heavy load to carry. Oh what a shame to needlessly bear the heartache of sorrow and pain. The I Am That I Am has offered to trade your agonies and tears for peace everlasting and joy overflowing. What an exchange! Gladly trade your insufficiency for His sufficiency. All you need to do is to let go and trust Him.

Understanding his own inadequacy, Moses was reassured that the all-sufficient one, The I Am That I Am, would be with him as he led the Israelites out of Egypt. Knowing that inquiring persons would ask who put him in charge and assigned him with such a mission, Moses questioned God concerning how he was to respond. Let them know that the God of your fathers has sent you, was God's reply. But, Moses was looking for a name that God was called by. And that name was I Am That I Am. "And Moses said unto God. Behold, when I come unto the children of Israel, and shall say unto them, The God of your fathers hath sent me unto you; and they shall say to me, What is his name? What shall I say unto them? And God said unto Moses, I Am That I Am: and he said, Thus shalt thou say unto the children of Israel, I AM hath sent me unto you." Exodus 3:13-14

Called by the name, I Am That I Am, identified Him as the one and only Supreme Being. Only He cannot be refrained, nor contained. No one but He, has no restraints. No matter can control Him because He controls all matter. Since He is the master of time and He occupies all of space, He is cannot be restricted to a certain time nor a specific place.

No sphere can contain His presence. No place exists where He cannot be found. David acknowledged that wherever he went, the presence of the Lord followed him. "Whither shall I go from thy spirit? Or whither shall I flee from thy presence? If I ascend up into heaven, thou art there: if I make my bed in hell, behold, thou art there. If I take the wings of the morning, and dwell in the uttermost parts of the sea; Even there shall thy hand lead me, and thy right hand shall hold me." Psalm 139:7-10 Whatever direction that David could turn, no path would lead him away from the spirit of the Lord. The earth is filled with the presence of the Lord. Neither can the heavens contain Him. "The heaven and heaven of heavens cannot contain him" 2 Chronicles 2:6 Whether you are walking from the ends

116

of the earth, or an astronaut floating is space, you may call upon the Lord, and from wherever you are, you will find Him. "The Lord is nigh unto all them that call upon him, to all that call upon him in truth." Psalm 145:18

I Am, I Am translated, I Know, I Know. All knowledge and understanding abides within Him. The entire universe cannot contain the vastness of His knowledge. He knows all, sees all, and hears all. He knows you well enough that He even knows the number of hairs upon your head. Whether one fall out or turns gray, He knows that too. "O Lord, thou has searched me, and known me. Thou knowest my downsitting, and mine uprising, thou understandest my thought afar off." Psalms 139:1-2 He even takes notice of when you sit down or stand up, and knows what thoughts that you are thinking. Not a word that you speak, that He does not know. He also knows every evil word spoken against you, and every evil attack planned against you. Thankfully, He knows how to combat every planned assault on you and your family. Not only does He know how, but He also knows when.

Immeasurable is His wisdom. "Great is our Lord, and of great power: his understanding is infinite." Psalm 147:5 I Am That I Am implies I Am Wisdom, I Am Wisdom. Intelligence you may gain from all kinds of sources. Sitting in a classroom, studying books, you may become filled with knowledge galore. Lessons learned through the experiences of life may teach you many valuable things. But true wisdom comes from the Lord. "The fear of the Lord is the beginning of wisdom." Proverbs 9:10 The beginning of wisdom is having a godly reverence and respect of the Lord. You cannot draw water from a sand pit. A bucket full of water can only be drawn from a well of water. Neither can you obtain wisdom without going to He who is wisdom.

He spreads His feathers across all of creation and His knowledge reaches beyond any limits. Likewise His power and authority are not held by any boundaries either. All other powers that be are under subjection to His power. The I Am that I Am is ultimately in control. Nothing is too difficult for the Lord to perform. "Ah Lord God! Behold, thou hast made the heaven and the earth by thy great power and stretched out arm, and there is nothing too hard for thee." Jeremiah 32:17 Child bearing at the ripe old age of ninety was not even a stretch for Him. Sarah, who deemed the notion impossible, laughed when she heard the news that she would birth a son at such an age. God responded by questioning Abraham, saying, "Is any thing too hard for the Lord" Genesis 18:14 The answer was no, because that He is all-powerful. Along with His power, He also is all authoritive.

God's eternal existence was reflected by the name I Am That I Am. He always had been and always would be. Since His being is completely independent of any other source, nothing can change His nature. While all others have their being from God, He is God.

His name implies that all sufficiency is contained within Him. All sufficient is He at all times. Whatever you need, He will be. That name means He Is enough, and besides Him, you need nothing else. I Am, then fill in the blank, whatever you need Him to be He is.

In your despair, He is your hope.

"For thou art my hope O, Lord God: thou art my trust from my youth." Psalm 71:5

Expressing his confidence in the Lord, David rejoiced knowing in whom in had placed his hope. David's expectations were built on nothing but the Lord. Hopelessness would have engulfed David, without a steadfast hope in the Lord. Hope built on anything else is a false hope.

Genuine hope cannot be build upon a varying substance. Circumstances change sometimes from day to day, maybe even minute by minute. Therefore, hope built upon your circumstance will surely crumble. Fix your hope upon a sure foundation, the one who never changes, Jesus Christ.

While your close-knit family and well-meaning friends may come to your aid, lending all the assistance to you that they possible can, you cannot place your confidence in them. They have no more promise of tomorrow than you do. They may be just as hopeless as you. Springing forth with their best intentions, they may be unable to carry out their good-hearted plans. But God can always deliver. Never will there be a boisterous terrain that He cannot cross. Putting your trust in the Lord is hope built upon a solid foundation. I Am That I Am is a name that you can trust in!

In your lack, He is your provision.

" But my God shall supply all your need
according to his riches in glory by Christ
Jesus." Philippians 4:19

When the Israelites needed food in the wilderness, God
sent quail and manna for them to eat. When they
needed water, a rock was struck and out came water.
Provision was miraculously made! He is a God of
plenty, who knows no lack. His resources never run
dry.

Kingdom seekers have no need to worry about the
needs of the day. While the birds of the air are fed,
Jesus acknowledged that you are more valuable than
the birds. Just as the fields are clothed in beautiful
green grass arrayed with magnificent lilies, He will
clothe you. When seeking God is top priority of your
life, then your basic needs will be met. "But seek ye
first the kingdom of God, and his righteousness; and all
these things will be added unto you." Matthew 6:33

God's promise to supply your needs is not an open
checkbook. Maxing out your credit cards on a
spending frenzy does not obligate Him to miraculously
cover the charges.

In danger, He is your protection

"Because thou has made the Lord, which is
my refuge, even the most High, thy
habitation;

120

There shall no evil befall thee, neither shall any plague come nigh thy dwelling. For he Shall give his angels charge over thee, to keep thee in all thy ways." Psalms 91:9-11

All those who will make their dwelling place underneath the shadowing wings of Almighty God, have this promise of protection. You will not be overtaken by evil. Angels have been commanded to guard and keep you.

In your weakness, He is your strength.

"When I am weak, then am I strong." 2 Corinthians 12:10

You can never be made strong until you understand that you are a weak individual. Only when you see your own weakness will you step out of your own little box of self-sufficiency. You can only be girded in His strength after you have stripped away all of your prideful independence.

"I can do all things through Christ which strengtheneth me." Philippians 4:13

In the heat of the battle, the fire will not consume you. By His grace, He will strengthen you to stand, no matter what your circumstances may be. Then when time comes to move forward, He will strengthen you to walk. Through the strength of the Lord, you can accomplish whatever task is laid before you.

You are unable, He enables you

"For without me, ye can do nothing." John 15:5

Understand your own inability and rely upon His empowerment. When you let go of self-reliance and become completely God-reliant, you will stand in awe, and be amazed at the achievements wrought by you, through the power and might of The Lord. Recognize that all skills and abilities that you have came from Him. Without The Lord, you can do nothing.

He is your solid rock.

"The Lord is my rock, and my fortress, and my deliverer; my God, my strength, in whom I will trust; my buckler, and the horn of my salvation, and my high tower." Psalm 18:2

"From the end of the earth will I cry unto thee, when my heart is overwhelmed: lead me to the rock that is higher than I." Psalm 61:2

Get your feet out of sinking sand! Disbelief and fear will bog you down in the mud. Stand upon Jesus Christ, a solid foundation that never wavers. He is the rock that will leave you standing when all else is shaking. Yes, He is a rock that is higher and bigger than you or your circumstances.

When you feel defeated, God is victorious

"The Lord is a man of war: the Lord is his name. Pharaoh's chariots and his host hath he cast into the sea: his chosen captains also are drowned in the Red sea. The depths have covered them: they sank into the bottom as a stone." Exodus 15:3-4

With the Egyptians on their heels, the Israelites needed to cross the Red Sea. Defeat seemed to be eminent for the Israelites. Then God parted the waters allowing them to cross over on dry land. As the Egyptians tried to cross over the sea; the waters came back over them, causing destruction to fall upon the enemy. When defeat stood in their way, God made a clear path for the children of Israel. When they needed protection from the enemy, they were protected. The Israelites could not be denied victory, because I Am That I Am was on their side. He is a man of war that victoriously wars for His children. You too have victory when you call upon the name of the Lord and trust in Him.

He is your peace in the midst of your storm

"He maketh the storm a calm, so that the waves thereof are still." Psalm 107:29

Jesus lay fast asleep as He was aboard a ship with His disciples. Waves rolled over into the boat, filling it with water, as a fierce storm arose. Afraid that they would perish the fearful disciples awakened Jesus, who calmed the storm by speaking peace. "And he arose, and rebuked the wind, and said unto the sea. Peace be still. And the wind ceased, and there was a great calm." Mark 4:39

He quiets the troubled seas of your life, as well. Climb into His lifeboat and peacefully row along life's journey, safe and secure with Him at the helm.

Your load is heavy, His Yoke is Easy

"Come unto me, all ye that labor and are heavy laden, and I will give you rest. Take my yoke upon you, and learn of me; for I am meek and lowly in heart: and ye shall find rest unto your souls. For my yoke is easy, and my burden is light." Matthew 11:28-30

You will not find this rest in a good night of sleep, but a rest within your spirit from the cares and trials of life. His rest puts a sparkle in your eye, a spring in your step, and a cheerful song in your heart.

He wants to be your burden-bearer

"Casting all your care upon him, for he careth for you." 1 Peter 5:7

"Cast thy burden upon the Lord, and he shall sustain thee." Psalm 55:22

Accept His invitation to cast all of your burdens and cares upon Him. Do not cast your burdens unto the Lord, only to get up, retrieve your heavy load back upon yourself, and continue on your journey weighed down with a spirit of heaviness. Leave your burdens with Him and you can walk in a new freedom. Would you throw out a bag of rotten potatoes, only to gather them up again and bring back into your house? Then once you have thrown all of the rottenness of your life upon The Lord, don't round it all up again.

He is what Mama Ain't, He Can when Mama can't

As hard as you may try, you cannot be all things that your family needs at all times. The title of Mama rings a bell of love, caregiver, and servant to your young. But the name Mama cannot measure up to all sufficient and, all knowing. Perfection embodies the name of I Am That I Am, signifying one who is without fault, a name that Mama cannot live up to. Inabilities will hamper Mama from time to time, but He knows no impossibilities. Some things will be out of Mama's reach. Your loving arms will only go so far. No Mountain is too high, neither is any valley to low, nor no ocean to wide for His loving arms to reach. Hovering over your children every breath that they take from the cradle to the grave is impossible for Mama. But the presence of the Lord shall cover them all of their days. Mama, you may become weak and feeble, and fear may try to overtake you. But He is stronger than an ox, bolder than a lion, yet gentle as a lamb. Because of the I Am that I Am, you have nothing to fear. When you are in a quandary, not knowing what to do, you vigorously search for an answer. Mama, He is the answer!

Mama, you may feed you children a good tasty meal. But only He can feed their soul. On a cold winter's night, you may tuck them in bed, covering them with a warm blanket, as they lay their head upon a nice soft pillow. But warmth for their soul comes from Him. You may forgive them of little mischievous deeds. But cleansing the soul from sin, only He can do. He came to set the captive free.

When you come to the end of yourself, He will still be there in all of His splendor and glory. "Before the mountains were brought forth, or ever thou hadst formed the earth and the world, even from everlasting to everlasting, thou art God." Psalm 90:2   His sovereignty had no beginning, neither does it have an ending. "But thou art the same, and thy years shall have no end." Psalm 102:27   He is the God of your past, the God of your now and the God of your future. The infinite I Am that I am is the lifeline at the end of your rope.

No false God can be called by the name I Am that I Am.   No other can acclaim to be all-powerful, all-knowing and ever present. The Lord Almighty is the only one who can meet you at any time and any place. No idol God can turn the ugly darken ashes of a life, which is in shambles, into a stunning life of beauty. But the one who is called I Am that I am will turn your ashes into sparkling diamonds. Worship to an idol will not restore a wretched broken soul. But with The Lord as your shepherd, He will refresh and restore, making you whole. The I Am that I Am is the only one who was dead and now is alive forevermore!

Who is watching your children?   The keeper of the moon, sun, stars, and the planets has an ever-watchful eye that never sleeps. With hands big enough to hold the entire universe, He will hold your family. If He feeds even the birds of the air, surely He will nourish your little flock. Those who make up your family circle can be trusted into the care of Him, who is called I Am That I Am, meaning He Is, He Is and always will be! Amen.

Chapter Ten

Now I Lay Me Down To Sleep

Mama, you could not face a more heart wrenching tragedy than the death of a child. The anguish of your horrendous loss seems to engulf your every thought, squeezing the life right out of you. Gone now is a child that was birthed from your very being, which you held ever so tightly in your bosom, one that you loved more than life itself. All the hopes and dreams that you had for this beloved child are replaced with a heart filled with pain and sorrow, leaving you in total desperation.

Paralyzed by the devastating loss, overwhelmed by sheer grief, yet life must continue on. Each new day is another challenge that you simply would rather not face. Day after day, a deeper pain in your heart and another bucket of tears seems to be all that life has to offer. As years go by, you are left with a longing in your heart, a void that cannot be filled. But there is one, who is able to comfort you and soothe your pain. "And I will pray the Father, and he shall give you another Comforter, that he may abide with you for ever." John 14:16 A distinct characteristic of the Holy Spirit is comforter. He, as your comforter will hold you in your darkest hour. As you cry a river of tears, He stands by to wipe every tear. He wants to heal your broken heart and fill it with peace and joy. As you lean upon Him, He will help you to cope with your loss, and you will find reason to live again.

Mom, if you have the assurance that your beloved child is in heaven with the Lord, then rest in peace. The

Lord has laid your precious one down to sleep. As their soul rest in peace, allow the presence of the Lord to rest your spirit as well. He will calm your troubled waters; give you courage in place of fear, and hope in place of hopelessness.

Every child of God has a hope beyond the grave. Death is a passageway, which leads beyond the gates of pearl, to a city, where the walls are made of jasper and garnished with magnificent stones. Running through the city is a grand and glorious street paved with gold. As the natural body takes its last breath, life as known on this earth has ended. But, that is the beginning of real living for the Christian. They have entered into the presence of Jesus Christ to live with Him eternally in heaven, where you can join them one day. That precious loved one of yours has simply fallen asleep in the mortal body. But, will awake in a new place with a new body. While death may have separated you, take courage in knowing that this is a temporary separation. Visualize them standing along side of Jesus welcoming you into heaven, once you take your stroll down that passageway called death.

Any old rundown shack used to be a brand new home. But, once torn down that house will never exist again. After the demise of the building, memories are all that the family has left of the old homestead. Housing the soul and spirit of any individual is the body in which they dwell. The house decays away, but the soul and spirit will continue to live forever. You may only have memories for the moment, but reunion day is coming. Rising one day to meet the Lord in the air, the soul will be garnished with a new house, clothed in a new body.

While this does not satisfy the longing and craving to hold and nurture that child in the present, you must look to the hope of the future.

Scripture confirms that a time does come to depart from this life. "a time to be born and a time to die." Ecclesiastes 3:2 Just as surely as a baby is born, one day that same person will also die. This time comes in a host of different ways and at different ages. Some people will have a very short time upon this earth, while others may have many long years in this life.

Great sorrow will bring a season of weeping and mourning. But, joy and laughter shall return again. "A time to weep, and a time to laugh; a time to mourn, and a time to dance." Ecclesiastes 3:4 Healing your broken spirit comes through both avenues. Tears of sadness are like a release valve. Left bottled up inside, the stress of your pain and the grief of your emotions will drain the life out of you. Joy and laughter must come on the heels of weeping and mourning. Laughter does the heart good like a healing ointment to the soul. But, the spirit that stays broken will decay away. Therefore, laughter is good for the mind, spirit and body. "A merry heart doeth good like a medicine: but a broken spirit drieth the bones." Proverbs 17:22

A tragic accident claimed the life of a young man several years ago. For some time, his parents were completely consumed by their grief. Heartache was their constant companion. About one full year after this horrific loss, the father laughed at something funny, for the first time since loosing his son. He actually felt guilty that he could find humor in anything.

131

After all, wasn't it downright disrespectful to enjoy life again, or so he felt. The truth is that the time for laughter had finally come. Certainly times of weeping have come and gone throughout the years. But, they now have times of laughter as well. They relish in the cherished memories of that beloved son with sadness at times. And at other times they joyfully reminisce about the happy times they enjoyed with him. By the grace of God, through the tears and times of laughter these parents have been restored to wholeness.

They take comfort and hope in the blessed assurance that their dear son is with the Lord. Knowing that the family circle will be reunited, as they enjoy the eternal presence of the Lord, makes the bliss of heaven even sweeter. Death has separated this family, but only for a season. A day is coming that death itself can no longer keep loved ones parted, so long as each one has a relationship with Jesus Christ. Such hope brings gladness in times of sorrow.

Mama could not fix the broken body of her son. But, the Holy Spirit could be a healing balm unto her broken heart. She chose to allow the Holy Spirit to comfort her, rather than shutting Him out. A closed window cannot welcome in the radiance of the sunshine. Neither can a closed heart receive in the warmth of peace and joy that the Holy Spirit so desperately longs to bring. "He healeth the broken in heart, and bindeth up their wounds." Psalm 147:3 As agonizing as it may be, open up your wounded heart to the Lord, and allow Him to restore you.

Grief, which comes in a series of stages, denial, anger, guilt or blame, depression and finally acceptance, is a normal outlet from your pain. God will help you through the excruciating pain as you muddle through each stage. Knowing what to expect in each stage will help to guide you through this process.

Denial

Upon hearing the tragic news, a devastating blow may send you spinning into a state of shock. Impossible to grasp hold of reality, your emotions cannot perceive what your ears are hearing, as you cry in anguish, this cannot be. The denial stage many times will pass quickly, and then comes the harsh facts of reality.

In disbelief, Peter, one of Jesus disciples, experienced the denial stage upon hearing the news that Jesus was to be put to death. "Then Peter took him, and began to rebuke him, saying, Be it far from thee, Lord: this shall not be unto thee." Matthew 16:22 Denying the facts was much easier than facing the truth.

Reeling and rocking, riding the shock waves of the moment, carrying you into a brief period of total disbelief is quite normal. However, living in a world of pretense, making believe that this never happened is another matter to reckon with. Loosing touch with reality by means of such deception is unhealthy. This sort of trickery on your mind hinders you from moving forward. Your pain is swallowed up in a deeper hole, by ignoring the facts. Painful as it may be, healing cannot come without dealing with the issues at hand.

Anger

Anger moves in, leaving you in the most vulnerable position to speak words or take action, which will bring you regrets latter. Quite frankly, the anger stage becomes an open door to temptation. "Be sober, be vigilant; because your adversary the devil, as a roaring lion, walketh about, seeking whom he may devour:" 1 Peter 5:8 Anger has a way of robbing you of sound mind, henceforth, letting your guard down. Then the roaring lion sees you as a feeble prey. Before long, he slyly moves in and attacks.

Be ye angry, and sin not: let not the sun go down upon your wrath." Ephesians 4:26 Cautiously be angry, not allowing your anger to become sinful, and be sure to get over your anger quickly. In other words, hurry up, and close the door to temptation. The longer anger resonates within you, the more apt, that you are to commit a sin. Anger will take you down a path. First comes resentment, and then bitterness is around the next little curve. Approaching the next block, you will discover hate and unforgiveness. Walking down this path not only allows sin to creep in, but also will torment your mind, turning you into a bigger emotional wreck that you were.

Since everyone in the family has suffered a loss, they too are going through the stages of grief. The atmosphere is tense, nerves are shaken, and emotions are raw for everyone. Therefore the anger stage presents a real potential for family disputes, causing hurt feelings, or possibly a major family conflict. Remember that everyone is dealing with their own pain as they work through their grief. Not everyone will move along at the same pace, neither will they all grieve in the same manner. The quicker that each one can overcome the anger stage, the sooner that the window of opportunity is closed on family squabbles.

Put the brakes on anger, before it breaks you. Harboring anger hinders the healing and mending of your broken heart. Like a sledgehammer, anger hammers at your heart, driving the pain and anguish deeper and deeper. Weighing you down with a much heavier load, anger adds a little more gloom to each day, each step becomes a little harder to walk, and each breath a little harder to breathe. Peace, joy and contentment cannot move into a heart that is filled with anger.

Danger up ahead! Anger left running rampant can become anger vented toward God. Nothing is wrong with expressing your hurts and disappointments to Him. But be careful that anger does not drive you into a state of rebellion against God. Worse yet, that your anger does not override your faith, leading to doubt and unbelief. Faith will drive you into God's loving arms, waiting to hold and console you. Turning you away from His peace and comfort, anger will cause you more turmoil and pain.

Allow your anger to become constructive instead of destructive. Many good organizations have been formed as the result of someone's anger being the fuel that ignited the flame. Many wonderful support groups exist today that were started by hurting people determined to help others. The burning desire to reach out to others many times was sparked by anger.

Loosing her daughter as a result of drug abuse, one Mama prayed that something good would evolve out of her tragic loss. Not wanting her daughter's death to be in vain, she prayed asking that God would use her misfortune as a tool to help someone else. Being involved in prison ministry, this Mother has been able to tell her story to inmates, who were struggling with drug addiction. Venting her anger in a positive manner, she is quite certain, that she has made an impact on others.

Guilt /Blame

Someone must be at fault. Questions and more questions began. Could I be the guilty one? How could I have prevented this? I should have protected them better. If I had done that, this would not have happen. You actually feel guilty that God did not take you instead. Running wild your imagination weighs you down with a heavy burden of guilt, when you are completely innocent. This saga continues until you have finally beaten yourself unmercifully.

Death is a natural occurrence, not the fault of your wrongdoing. This may be better understood in the case of some illness or disease. But what about an accident caused possibly by your own human error. Jesus Christ was the only perfect human who ever walked on this earth. Cautious as you may be, accidents will still happen. As difficult as it may be, you must stop torturing yourself before your brokenness can begin to heal.

If you are not at fault, then surely someone must be. Lifting the guilt off of your shoulders can easily make way for the blame game to begin. Justified or not, if you search long enough, you will probably find a direction to point your finger. Stirring this pot only stirs up more wounds to be mended and more anger to work through.

Concerning a man that had been blind from his birth, the disciples once questioned Jesus, who had sinned that caused this man to be blind, the man or his parents. Jesus responded that neither he nor his parents had sinned. No one was to blame for his blindness. But, God was going do manifest His work through this boy's blindness. Bad things happen to good people in not just a cliché, but a true statement. Sometimes there simply is no one at fault.

Guilt will have your head hung in shame at the thought of enjoying anything pleasurable. Hobbies that you once enjoyed should be continued, not placed on a back shelf. Exploring new avenues of enjoyment may just kindle a new spark of life, which you desperately need. You should make your best effort to enjoy living once again. Jesus desires to give you a life that is abundantly full and rich. Indulging in your favorite activities, enjoying moments of laughter, pursuing your hopes and dreams in not disgraceful, neither disrespectful. But, shameful it would be to crawl into a shell, never to enjoy life again.

Depression

Usually along with the realization of reality comes a time of depression. In your devastation, you feel all alone. Life seems to be nothing but a deep, dark, empty hole. Your mind may be so captured by your loss that you cannot even think clearly. Daily chores must be put on hold, because you cannot function in your normal routine.

As you mourn the loss of your child, there seems to be no beauty to behold. All of life looks dark and gloomy. Even a gorgeous sunrise cannot brighten your day. And at the end of the day a magnificent sunset only brings another night of emptiness. A garden of lovely flowers may be completely meaningless. Unnoticed to your tear filled eyes will be the beauty of a rainbow arrayed in an assortment of bright, bold colors. Birds singing in beautiful harmony will offer no music to your ears.

The Mom, who had lost her son in an accident, vividly remembers the very first time that she walked outside and the beauty of the day caught her attention. Brilliant clouds adorned the sky above. Bringing a little ray of cheer into her heart was the bright sunshine. Freshness filled the air, like she had not sensed in quite awhile. Her recognition of a lovely day symbolized a relief from the depression that had gripped her. This does not mean that she never had another depressed day. But, not every day was gloomy. Brighter days were on the horizon.

During this time of depression, weeping until you have exhausted all of your energy will make up many of your days. Though the river of tears seems to be endless, do not hold back. Cry until you can't cry anymore. God gave a wonderful gift when He made tears. Tears shed from your eyes will be a healing ointment to your broken heart. Holding back the tears will be like withholding a healing salve.

Short periods of isolating yourself from others may be beneficial. Of course you need time to reflect on precious moments of the past, as well as looking toward the future. Sorting out your feelings and collecting your thoughts are part of the process of moving forward. However, for most people a long period of seclusion is unhealthy.

Equally important will be times of family and friends gathering around to offer their condolence and support. You now have someone to express your feelings with. Talking out your pain can be just as healing as the crying stage. At the death of Lazarus, the brother of Mary and Martha, they had comfort from their friends. "And many of the Jews came to Martha and Mary, to comfort them concerning their brother." John 11:19

Take control over your thoughts instead of allowing your thoughts to control you. Channel thoughts of your loved one into precious memories, rather than trying to suppress those memories. Those memories are in you consciousness and you will either deal with them or they will torment you. So deal with them in a positive manner. Laugh at those hilarious moments of the past. The Mom and Dad who lost their son now laugh at funny things he did while he was alive. However, a good cry sometimes is still in order. You may laugh some days and cry on others. Both laughter and tears are healing virtues.

His Mother shared with me that she envisions her son being in a little box, which is fashioned inside of her heart. Each day she goes into her heart, pulls out the little box and opens it. She then has her reflection time, reflecting back on memories of her son. During this time, she talks about him, converses of things that she would like to share with him, if he were here. After a few moments, she then closes the box back up, stores it away inside her heart, where she will return the next day for her few moments of quiet time, her reflection time. Reflecting upon him, expressing her innermost feelings and basking in his memories is soothing to Mama's heart. In this manner, she is constantly open to her emotions, rather than suppressing them.

Private devotion time with just you and the Lord must not be neglected. "In thy presence is fullness of joy." Psalm 16:11 Soaking in the radiance of His love, can open up a floodgate of joy over your soul, even in the midst of great sorrow. Feasting on His word feeds the emptiness of your hungry soul. As you relish in His love, an unexplainable peace will warm your heart. "Thou wilt keep him in perfect peace, whose mind is stayed on thee: because he trusteth in thee." Isaiah 26:3 Staying in the presence of the Lord will keep you in a place of peace.

Acceptance

This journey has brought you through the roughest seas that you have ever sailed. Accepting the harsh facts seems much more than is humanly possible. However, this acceptance stage is the vital link connecting you back to your life and your purpose. Like a revolving door that never closes, acceptance becomes a spinning circle that never stops. Sparked by a tiny flicker of acceptance, the desire to continue living grows a little more. Each small step forward moves you toward another little ember of acceptance.

A lighted candle in a darken room will shine a little light, removing a small amount of darkness. A second candle will show forth a little more light, and a little less blackness. Such as with the dark, weary, broken heart, each ray of light is another glimmer of hope. Each time that you reach a new level of acceptance, the strength to continue on, grows as well, and the cycle continues. This process may continue throughout the rest of your life.

Much wasted time and energy can be used trying to understand why. Life never offers an explanation to some things. Reserve this energy for learning to cope and coming to terms with your loss. Acceptance does not mean that you understand why. Many times, trying to rationalize and comprehend, trying to absorb it all in leaves you in a pile of confusion, instead of giving you answers. Through faith in Jesus Christ, in spite of your loss and fears, you can get up and find a reason to go on with life.

Challenging will be the upheavals of your emotions. Understanding the different stages of the process of grief may help you to sort through some of your perplexity. These stages may not necessarily come in the order that they have been described. Quite frankly, you may experience one or all of the stages more than once. As each stage arises, deal with it and then move on. Each stage is a natural method of healing and restoration to a hurting heart.

A sword seems to pierce through your heart as you stand by the grave where your child has been laid. No towel is big enough to dry all of your tears. Nothing but despair and gloom fills the air. You wonder how you will find the strength to take the next step. But Mama, that grave offers hope. Because of the death and resurrection of Jesus Christ, life everlasting lies on the other side of the grave to all who believe upon Him. As you stand and weep tears of sorrow, your loved one is resting peacefully in the arms of Jesus.

One day you will join that precious loved one along with the host of other believers around the throne of God. Ringing throughout the heavens, voices of praise, singing songs of victory can be heard. Jubilant rejoicing forever and ever will be. Not a tear to be found, as all sadness is wiped away. But, until then sleep on my child.

Chapter Eleven

When Mama needs fixing

Most Mothers would rather bare the burden of suffering than to watch her children suffer. Willing to suffer the consequences herself, many times a Mother has thrown herself into great danger protecting her young from some horrible tragedy. Through sickness, pain, heartache, or hardships of any kind, Mama would gladly exchange places with her children if only she could. But, the flip side of that coin is accompanied by a set of woes all of its own. Mama with small children to rear, challenged by major health issues in her own life is not easy either.

A severe back injury forever changed the life of my own Mother when I was only eight years old. As a young Mother of three ranging in ages two through eleven, excruciating pain forbid her from performing normal daily activities. Heartbroken, she felt somewhat hindered in caring for her family. However, through her love, thoughtfulness and sheer determination, Mama enriched our lives more than she ever imagined.

Weeks at a time were spent with Mama in the hospital during the formative years of her children. Undergoing several surgeries and wrenching with piercing pain became a way of life for many of her years. Added to the physical pain was the grief of being away from her girls. Although she knew that we were in good hands with our grandparents, her heart was still burdened that she was not the one taking care of her little ones. Granny would always have a meal prepared where

143

Daddy would come to eat and spend a few minutes with us after work each day, and then on to the hospital to visit Mama.

After the hospital stay, recuperation time usually meant bed rest for an extended amount of time. Although she was always thankful to be home, at times her heart grew very heavy because that she could not fulfill the list of things that she longed to do for her family. Places to go, which she had to miss, sometimes brought a tear to her eye. If anyway possible, she would muster up all the strength that she had, in order to attend any special event involving her girls. During our school days, a Mother-Daughter banquet was held at school each year around Mother's Day. No matter how much pain she endured, Mama never missed sitting at the table, partaking of the banquet with her daughters.

Mama could not run, play ball, or ride a bicycle with us, yet she found ways to play and enjoy entertainment with her little girls. She enjoyed playing board games, such as monopoly, sorry and checkers. Now that I am much older, I realize that her pleasure came from spending time playing with her children more than the games she played. Mama was determined that her ill health would not rob her of quality time spent with her family. Playing games certainly presented another teaching opportunity. Since my younger sister always cheated, she had to be taught to play fairly.

Of course, Mama could not complete household duties until her back had some mending time and she became steadier on her feet. Not only was my Mama a fabulous cook, but also she thoroughly enjoyed cooking. Imagine the horror of a great chef lying in bed sending inexperienced girls to the kitchen. In the beginning my oldest sister did the cooking and I was the dishwasher. Somehow it took me much longer to clean up the mess than it did for her to cook the meal. After awhile I learned to cook too, this proved to be quite interesting. Learning to cook for me meant getting instructions from the bedside of Mama. After step one was completed, I would run back to the bed seeking advice on what to do next. You see, Mama's recipes were all tucked away inside her head, not to be found in a recipe book. Measuring out a cup or a tablespoon or maybe a teaspoon was easy enough. But learning to decipher between the measurements of a pinch of this, or just a little bit of that, or just a dab was a little more difficult. Once Mama was stirring again, much more variety was added to the menu. Even deserts were included. Mama did not cook very many meals that did not end with a delicious cake, pie, or maybe a banana pudding. She even made us homemade cookies and at Christmastime an assortment of candies that she hand made was always readily available at our house.

Along with cooking other household chores fell upon us girls to do as well, which Mama felt very badly about. Dusting, sweeping, mopping, scrubbing and laundry were chores shared between my sisters and me. About the laundry, a few items may have gone into the washing machine one color and came out a different color. While Mama sometimes felt sad maybe even a little guilty that she could not perform these task, she did not realize the value of the responsibilities her girls were learning. She was very adequate in teaching her children.

Discipline was another job that Mama did very adequately. Quite frankly, I believe that my Mama invented time-out. My younger sister was a bit too young to get involved in the sibling rivalry that sometimes sprung up between my older sister and me. In an effort to end our spats, Mama would send us to the couch, making us sit on opposite ends and not to speak a word until she told us that we could. While my sister has a long list of good attributes, no matter how hard you search that list, you will not find the word quiet. Consequently, our stay on the couch was extended more than a few times. The worst punishment came when time was up and we were finally allowed to get up off the couch. Mama made us hug each other and say the three most dreaded words "I am sorry."

Another method of discipline used by Mama was giving a stern harsh stare of the eyes. Never will I forget an incident that happened when I was a very small child that brought that staring look of disapproval to Mama's face. My Big Papa was the pastor of the small church that we attended. One Sunday morning Mama was not feeling well. (This was before the back injury.) She decided that staying home from church would raise some concern and even worry to Big Mama and Big Papa that she was sick. Not wanting to distress them, off to church we went. As Big Papa stood in the pulpit about to pray, a wise thought ran through my childish mind. Certain that if he prayed for Mama she would be well, I ran to the pulpit, standing on tip toes, with outstretched arms, pulling on the hem of his suit coat. Bending over to my level, he listened as I whispered into his ear to pray for Mama because she was sick.

As I turned to go back to my seat next to Mama, the entire congregation was roaring with laughter, except my Mama. Seeing the frown upon her face and the glaring vicious look which penetrating all the way through me, I quickly made an about face and ran over to sit by my Aunt, who was in stitches with laughter.

When service was over that morning another Aunt came to my rescue. She cleverly convinced Mama not to punish me because I had acted out of love and concern for her. No other punishment was necessary, because the evil cutting of the eyes had been sufficient. Unfortunately, I must admit that was not the last time that I ever witnessed that gleaming, staring look from Mama. She seemed to always know how to gain my attention and demand a change of behavior by the horrifying look that she so well expressed in her eyes.

Of all that Mama ever has been in my life or anything that she ever did for me, I am most grateful for the Christian principals that she faithfully instilled within me. Not only did she teach me the word of God by her mouth, but more importantly, day-by-day she lived her life accordingly. In other words, she lived what she preached. Until her dying day her life was guided by the word of God. Teaching me more than the Ten Commandments and bible stories such as Adam and Eve, Noah's Ark, David and Goliath, or Jonah and the whale, she showed me what it meant to have a real genuine love for Jesus Christ. Walking by a steadfast faith in the Lord was so well modeled by the walk of my Mama.

Many times Mama could not get to church on Sundays. But, her sickness would not hinder her girls from the house of God. Mama made sure of that. Whether Mama was up and going with us, or whether she was hospitalized, or if she was home and unable to attend, my sisters and I were always in church on Sundays. For every Sunday school teacher that taught me and every sermon I heard preached, I am thankful. Oh how grateful I am for and all those hymns and chorus that I learned. Not only did they touch me then, but my soul is still moved and my spirit uplifted by humming an old tune that I learned as a child. But, I am most appreciative to my Mama because she made certain that I was there. Today almost any given Sunday will find all three of Mama's girls is church, worshipping God.

Another great lesson learned from Mama was that of perseverance. Refusing to allow a sick bed to hold her down, Mama never gave up. Instead she always bounced back. When lying in bed would have been much easier, she pushed and pulled herself up. When each step was a struggle and pain ripped through her with each stride, she refused to be confined to a wheelchair. Although, in later years she had to resort to the wheelchair, she still managed to overcome that chair time and time again. Therefore, her children learned not to quit just because an obstacle gets in the way. Side step that mountain, climb over it, or better yet pray until it crumbles, Mama taught us to press on, stay the course, and fulfill our ambitions. However, she also encouraged us to seek the will of God in all of our endeavors, knowing that if we were in His will that He would see us through until the end.

Mama taught us the art of gratitude. Instead of dwelling on her pain, she focused her attention upon her blessings. Countless number of times, we heard nothing but praise coming out of her mouth, thanking God for His goodness to her and for bringing her through each trying time. "In everything give thanks: for this is the will of God in Christ Jesus concerning you." 1 Thessalonians 5:18 In pain and turmoil, Mama gave thanks, not for the pain, but for the grace of God to strengthen her. In the midst of each storm, she knew that God had a silver lining behind each cloud. She thanked God for the rainbow, which she knew was around the bend. Her most famous saying is found in these words "if you will look around, you will find someone worst off than you." As her heart went out to them in pity, another item was added to her thankful list, being grateful that her condition was not any worse.

Sharing in the burden of friends and neighbors and helping to lighten their load was another wonderful example Mama set for us girls. She would call to check up on an ailing neighbor and assure them that she would be praying for their recovery. Sometimes she would ask one of us girls to make the call if she did not feel like talking. Many times we have come home from school and she had made a dish to carry to someone whose family had been struck with illness or maybe even death. And then there were those times that she

149

was not up to the challenge and she would ask us to prepare the dish to carry. More was being accomplished than food being delivered to another home. The message of caring for others was being taught to her children.

What Mama saw as a stumbling block to fulfilling her Motherly duties was quite the opposite. Turning her trials into teaching techniques, she taught her girls many valuable lessons. Learning more than household responsibilities, we learned to care for one another. Learning to share as a family meant more than sharing toys or chores. We share in the grief and tears that may sometimes inflict a family member, as well as the joys that life sometimes will bring.

Love and commitment being the binding cord that holds a home together was not something that we learned from a fairytale in a storybook, nor some movie played out on the big screen. No writer could have penned a love story as sweet as the story of love that we saw between our Mother and Father. No actors could have played a love story as genuine as theirs. Of all that they taught us, perhaps this was the best lesson of all.

Of course, the hospital stays and the numerous Doctor visits took a toll on the family's budget. Thankfully, she was insured, but insurance did not cover the entire cost. Desperately yearning to give us more and better things, Mama was saddened even sometimes felt guilty that she had to say no to some of our petty wants. Well, truthfully we had all that we needed. We always had a roof over our head, food to eat, and clothes to wear. Since we grew up in an era before the school halls were lined with fashion designer clothes and sneakers attached with a one hundred dollar price tag were unheard of, we fit in quite well with all the others at school. However, we learned budgeting skills through this experience. Both of my parents were very diligent in making sure that all the bills got paid.

Mama never allowed her heath issues to cause any slackness in her parenting skills. While Mama had a back in need of mending, she never had a broken spirit. With a positive attitude and steadfast faith in the Lord, she faced each challenge that life brought her way, which taught her children good principles to live by. Though she tried to fix all that she could, she had a strong resolve to trust in the Lord for what she could not fix. Whatever situation she found herself in, she made the best of it.

"Who can find a virtuous woman? For her price is far above rubies." Proverbs 31:10 The woman of excellent character, good morals, strength and honor is far more valuable than any other treasure. My father found that woman when he found my mother. "Her children arise up, and call her blessed." Proverbs 31:28 Certainly both of my sisters and I would arise up and call my Mother blessed and we would emphatically declare to the world that we were truly blessed to have had her as our Mother.

Recently angels were summoned to her bedside, where they gathered her up and ushered her through the gates of pearl. Peacefully she left here, headed for her home above. Freely she may dance for joy as she strolls down a street laid with the finest pure gold. Never again will a tear be shed from her eye and never again will she be inflicted by pain. While she may have said goodbye, her memories will linger on. Lessons that she taught us are more treasured now than before. Not only have her three girls benefited from her teachings, but they have been passed on to the next generation as well.

Chapter Twelve

Standing Tall

Listen! Hear the rumblings of the noisy crowd as you shuffle through a mob of people. Stretching as far as you can, leaning to the right, and then to the left, trying to catch a glimpse of the sights up ahead as you inch your way through the massive crowd. With all of your maneuvering around, your view is masked over by a wall of bodies, and a ceiling of heads. Toddling along, a small child sees nothing but feet, while the muffled voices are nothing more than a sea of confusion. Like a little ant about to be trampled, this child feels even smaller now. Suddenly Daddy lifts his little one up above the crowd. Riding upon Daddy's shoulders, this little tot now feels ten feet tall. Not a care in the world as this little one sits high upon the world. Clearly unfolding are all the sights up ahead, and the sea of confusion disappears.

Trials of life many times may knock you to the ground, clipping your feet out from under you. With head bowed low, you try to crawl through the mass confusion, hitting your head against a brick wall with every turn. You can't see anyway out and you certainly can't see which way is up. Wishing that you could dig a tunnel to escape from it all, but you can't even find a shovel to use. Suddenly your heavenly Father scoops you up into His arms and lifts you upon His shoulders. Soaring above the chaos, you take a breath of fresh air, and you feel ten feet tall.

Precisely designed for the unique needs of His children, His shoulders come in different shapes and sizes, not always taking on the look that you were expecting to find. Formed specifically for you, His shoulder will always perfectly fit the need that you have at any given time. Never will you find that His shoulder has no room left for you to stand.

Looming over you is nothing but the sights and sound of discouragement. Oppressed from every side, your spirit is crushed, knocking the wind out from under your sails. The Father tenderly gathers you underneath His wing, and stands you up on the shoulder of an encouraging word. The Holy Spirit may whisper gentle words of peace into your spirit, or He may send a messenger along with words of hope.

Down and out, feeling puzzled and all alone, your chin dragging the ground, then someone comes along with an encouraging word, cheering you on. As courage takes root and begins to grow within you, your spirit begins to rise. Before long you are standing to your feet again, with your head held high. Courageously you meet the challenges that lie before you. Encouragement may come beaming at you from many different avenues.

Through their love, support and encouragement, oftentimes, the Lord uses your very own circle of family and friends to lift your spirit and stand you up tall again. In your dismay, a loving word spoken by a true friend may cause your wings to begin to flutter with new life. Distraught out of your mind, your friends may come to your rescue helping you to regain your focus. Your faith may even grow stronger through the prayers and faith of your family and friends. Buried in the arms of a trusted loved one, a good hug brings healing to a hurting soul and courage to a faint heart. A good familiar shoulder to cry upon has lifted a heavy load many times.

Interacting with others who have weathered the same storm that seemly will swallow you opens another door of encouragement. Sometimes your family and close friends may not have ever stood in your shoes. Therefore understanding your crisis is more than they can fathom. Searching for words of encouragement finds them at a total loss. At times like this, you may find that joining a support group may become a shoulder for you to stand upon. A swimming instructor must learn to swim before they can teach someone else. Clutching your arm, holding you up and helping you to rise above the turbulent sea, is someone who has already peddled through the same rough water that you now are treading through.

Your close contacts may express sympathy over your sorrows. They hurt for you, but lack the ability to relate to your circumstance. On the other hand, joining a support group connects you with others who truly know your situation. Having walked the same road that you are now traveling, they know exactly the pain that you feel. Instead of sympathy, they have empathy for you, meaning they actually know and understand your pain. They also know how to meet you where you are. When you think that your river cannot be crossed, find someone who has crossed that same river. Waiting on the other side of the riverbank is a puddle of encouragement. Begin to wade out into the puddle, then lie down and immerse yourself in the water, and courage will seep into your spirit.

Mingling amongst a crowd of strangers with a dear friend of mine, who was a cancer survivor, sometimes our path has crossed with another who was suffering the sting of cancer, or one who possibly had survived the ordeal as well. Upon learning the news of each other, even though they were strangers, their emotions immediately connected. Through their eyes, they each could read each other's story. Understanding between the two of them ran deeper because they each knew the difficulties that the other had faced. Each of them had experienced that dreaded visit to the Doctor, horrified as they received the earth shattering news of a cancer diagnosis. Both had suffered through the ravishing effects of chemotherapy. Someone who had never faced the challenging crisis of cancer could not understand the fear and uncertainty that had gnawed into the very core of their spirit. In a moment of solitude silence, a language was spoken between them that no other person in the room understood. Enduring the agony of defeat, only to rise above to the thrill of victory, had taught my friend well how to reach the next person on their level. That is the same benefit that joining a support group can offer if the need arises. Those in the group may not be able to change your circumstance, but they can take you by the arm and pull you up and help you to stand on your feet again.

While those surrounding you may strengthen and encourage you, sometimes you are still left searching for answers. The road ahead of you seems like a darken maze, as you crawl and grope your way through, each little turn carries you down another trail of bewilderment. A counseling session with your minister or a professional counselor may help to steer you upon a lighted path. Lifting the weight of perplexity off of your shoulder lifts your spirit, allowing you to stand a little taller. Contrary to what some would believe, seeking wise counsel is a bold and courageous act. Opening up and sharing your thoughts and sheer raw emotions with a neutral person takes real courage and strength.

Many times your family and close circle of friends are hurting too deeply from the crisis at hand to sort out their own feelings. Certainly trying to help you sort through your emotions is a bigger task than they are equipped to handle. The trained professional counselor unequivocally cannot match the love and moral support of your closest friends and family members. However, helping you to cope, your loved ones probably cannot match the skills of the counselor. Do not shy away from the wonderful results received from good sound godly council. "A wise man will hear, and will increase learning; and a man of understanding shall attain unto wise counsels" Proverbs 1:5 Seeking wise council can be like searching for a solid shoulder to stand upon.

Suppose that you get a thorn in your hand while touching and admiring a beautiful rose. Ouch! If the thorn is not removed, it will fester and become infected, causing more pain. The only relief is to pick and pluck away at the skin until the thorn comes out, which is even more painful than the initial sticking of the thorn. Much like a professional counselor, who may pull and pry to the bottom of your pain. But after the digging is done, the pain lessens. Trying to protect you from the necessary digging, your dearest loved ones will be more prone to soothe the pain with another ice pack, rather than getting to the thorn.

Many people who in the midst of their turmoil have sought out professional counsel were pleasantly surprised at the end result. While in a session with the counselor they cried and poured out their inner being. Quite frankly, the digging was painful. But, they walked out of the office feeling like a heavy load had been lifted. They would go back and the digging may have even been deeper, but they sensed a greater relief. Each visit with the counselor helped to lighten the heart a little more, allowing them to stand a littler taller.

Another set of broad shoulders to stand upon can be found by joining ranks with other believers. Those that you worship with week after week, taking you under their wings, covering you with prayer, is truly powerful. In prison Peter lay sleeping between two guards as he was bound with chains. Thank God, Peter had a praying church. "Peter therefore was kept in prison: but prayer was made without ceasing of the church unto God for him." Acts 12:5 As a result of all the prayers, an angel came forth rescuing Peter, releasing him from the chains that once held him captive. The prayers of his church family literally stood Peter up on his feet, delivering him from bondage, as he walked out in a brand new freedom.

Assaulted, bruised and battered, you may feel the wind of the walls as they come crashing down on top of you, leaving you buried underneath all the rubble. You cannot even gather up enough strength to remove all of the debris, much less to stand. You can't even crawl. Then the faithful saints of your congregation rally around you, showering you with love, speaking words of faith into your ear, and lifting you up in prayer. Their prayers are powerful enough to remove the rubble, stand you up on your feet, and send waves of courage running up and down your spine.

Wonderful it is to combine your worship with others and to benefit from their concerted prayers, but nothing can replace your own private devotion time with the Lord. A good quality moment in the presence of the Lord can refresh and renew like nothing else can. Never will you stand any taller than when you are on a bended knee in prayer. Budding with new life, your wilted spirit will blossom as you spend time in prayer and reading His word. New life will be breathed into your spirit through His word, because His word is alive. His word is truth and the truth will stand you up while deception will let you fall. Quiet time in His word is a perfect setting for the Holy Spirit to breathe new life and fresh strength unto you. Through your prayers, take time to worship Him, bring your request unto Him, and listen for His voice to speak. Many times, a spotlight is shone upon a clear path leading you out of the trail of bewilderment, through His written word, as well as a word spoken into your heart. Listen for His words of comfort, joy, peace and instruction. You will then be rejuvenated, revived and ready to move forward.

No man is an island. Regardless of the method you use for your encouragement and consolation, find someone or a group to help you during difficult times. Do not try to climb every mountain or swim every ocean alone. The bible instructs us to love one another, encourage one another and to help bear each other's burdens. "Bear ye one another's burdens." Galatians 6:2 God designed us to lean upon each other. Facing each challenge, fighting through every crisis, and carrying all of your burdens alone steps outside of the perimeters set by God. Turning a deaf ear to an encouraging word, or a word of wisdom, or refusing consolation may very well be refusing a steady shoulder to stand upon.

Although the support offered by family, friends and fellow worshipers is wonderful and uplifting, you must not totally depend on sailing through life propped up on others. You must learn to stand in the power of the Lord. "Finally, my brethren, be strong in the Lord, and in the power of His might. Put on the whole amour of God that ye may be able to stand against the wiles of the devil." Ephesians 6:10-11 Armed and ready for battle stand in the strength and courage of the Lord. Out of his corner comes the enemy, with arrows flying in all directions. Oh, but standing in your corner is the victorious one, quenching every fiery dart. Gird yourself up in the amour of God and you will never stand-alone. But ever so tall you will stand.

Stand firmly in a positive attitude. You will never be the life of a pity party, because pity will sap the life right out of you. Taking your problems down a trail of

160

pity will bury you deeper in the mud, while allowing your problems to take you down a highway of praise, will keep you dancing along the way. The longer that you wallow in your self-pity, the more pitiful you will become, while the more you praise, the more positive outlook you will enjoy.

Trying to mend all the broken fences surrounding your family, you become tired and weary. As soon as you get one side of the fence fixed, another side is torn down. Sometimes you just need a shoulder to lean upon and rest. Mama you must take time to renew and refresh yourself. Rest is vital for the well being of your body, soul, and spirit. A worn out mule cannot plow as efficiently as a fresh one can. Neither can a worn out Mama carry the load of her family as effectively as when she is rested and fresh. When you are slumped over with weariness, a little relaxation will stand you up straight and tall again.

Each time that you get knocked down, climb upon a set of big broad shoulders. Ride high on top of the world, instead of being trampled by a heavy load. Oh yes, Mama needs a shoulder to lean upon, one to cry upon, and one that stands ten feet tall. Mama cannot afford missed opportunities to be encouraged and strengthened. Because Mama, more times than you can imagine your shoulder will be the one that God uses to stand your children up tall. Looking to Mama, they will come for encouragement, words of wisdom, peace and solace, strength and direction for the course of life.

As loving and rewarding as Motherhood may be, many trials, heartaches, and sufferings does come with the territory. Sometimes Mama, you use all the glue and plaster that you can find, and still cannot put all the pieces back together. When things are so broken that all the king's horses cannot mend them, don't despair. THE KING can fix it. That is the King of Kings and Lord of Lords, Jesus Christ. The fix will not on always be on your terms either. But His terms will always be for the greater good of all concerned.

Life is a journey of many twists and turns, ups and downs, where many of your sweet dreams are turned into sweet realities, yet others turned into bitter disappointments. At times you will sail on smooth clear waters, while at other times the waves of the turbulent seas will knock you down. Springing you back upon your feet again is a loving shoulder lent to you by the Lord. Then He calms the storm and gently whispers peace into your ear. After all the rowing and toiling has been done, no matter how rough the sailing may have been, if you and all of your family lands in heaven, then all has ended well.

LaVergne, TN USA
22 October 2010
201885LV00001BA/1/P